ACTING & AUD___ __NING FOR THE 21ST CENTURY

Acting & Auditioning for the 21st Century covers acting and auditioning in relation to new media, blue and green screen technology, motion capture, web series, audiobook work, evolving livestreamed web series, and international acting and audio work. Readers are given a methodology for changing artistic technology and the global acting market, with chapters covering auditions of all kinds, contracts, the impact of new technology, and issues relating to disabled actors, actors of color, and actors that are part of the LGBTQIA community.

Stephanie Barton-Farcas is the Founder and Artistic Director of Nicu's Spoon Theater Company (www.spoontheater.org), based in New York City and Hawaii. She is also the co-founder of the Disability in Cinema Coalition and sits on the board of Identity Theater Company. She is the author of a previous book, *Disability & Theatre: A Practical Manual for Inclusion in the Arts* (Routledge, 2017).

ACTING &
AUDITIONING FOR
THE 21ST CENTURY

TIPS, TRENDS, AND TECHNIQUES FOR FILM,
STAGE, DIGITAL AND NEW MEDIA

Stephanie Barton-Farcas

Routledge
Taylor & Francis Group

NEW YORK AND LONDON

First published 2019
by Routledge
711 Third Avenue, New York, NY 10017

and by Routledge
2 Park Square, Milton Park, Abingdon, Oxon, OX14 4RN

Routledge is an imprint of the Taylor & Francis Group, an informa business

© 2019 Taylor & Francis

The right of Stephanie Barton-Farcas to be identified as author of this work has been asserted by her in accordance with sections 77 and 78 of the Copyright, Designs and Patents Act 1988.

Library of Congress Cataloging-in-Publication Data
Names: Barton-Farcas, Stephanie, author.Title: Acting &
auditioning for the 21st century : tips, trends, and techniques for film,
stage, digital and new media / Stephanie Barton-Farcas.
Other titles: Acting and auditioning for the 21st century
Description: New York, NY : Routledge, 2018. | Includes
bibliographical references and index.
Identifiers: LCCN 2018019304| ISBN 9780815352112 (hardback) |
ISBN 9780815352129 (pbk.) | ISBN 9781351131551 (ebk) | ISBN
9781351131551 (Master)
Subjects: LCSH: Acting—Auditions. | Acting—Vocational guidance.
Classification: LCC PN2071.A92 B37 2018 | DDC 792.02/8—
dc23LC record available at https://lccn.loc.gov/2018019304

ISBN: 978-0-8153-5211-2 (hbk)
ISBN: 978-0-8153-5212-9 (pbk)
ISBN: 978-1-351-13155-1 (ebk)

Typeset in Bembo
by Florence Production Ltd, Stoodleigh, Devon

CONTENTS

FIGURES

ACKNOWLEDGMENTS

I have lived in both New York and Los Angeles and they each have their substantial place in the acting world. However, there is a vibrancy, a realness, a grit in New York City unmatched by anywhere on the planet (and I have travelled the globe). This book is dedicated to New York City and the many world class artists I adore who live and work there. You each know who you are.

Thanks to the actors who contributed quotes and stories for the book: James Morrison, Judith Ivey, Henry Winkler, the late John Ritter, Jeff Nichols, Rachel Handler, Lea Solonga, Tony Randall and Jack Klugman, the late Jerry Orbach, Anthony Sher, Akin Salawu, Dave Marantz, Stephanie Salvato Gould, C. Stephen Foster, Orlando Jones, the late Mel Blanc, Lisa Howard, Tim Robbins, William Esper, Marcus Geduld, Stephanie Gould, the late Sir Bryan O'Loghlan, the late Alfred Lunt, Linnea Berthelson, Laverne Cox, John Bell, and M.K. Lewis. If you do not know the actors and teachers quoted in this book, shame on you – look them up. They are working actors with long and respected careers. If you want to be like them, know your field.

Mostly though, this book is for my mom, my endless cheerleader. And for Nate, born again in Hawaii. Special love to Damon Law who designed the amazing book cover. To Maggie Lally – you know why.

INTRODUCTION

"I'd like to thank the Academy . . ."

How many of us have mouthed these words breathlessly staring into their bathroom mirror while clutching a hairbrush, shampoo bottle or other Oscar/Tony/Grammy stand-in? Many of us, I will bet. But let's break that down into the harsh reality. How many *only* dream of the accolades, the awards, the red carpets, the photo ops, the attention of screaming fans and the money? Most. How many, then, not only dream of the great accolades, but also the great parts, the classic roles, the film scenes, the stage rehearsals, the costumes, the sets, the smell of a set or a theater, the hard work itself. Much fewer. I hope that you are one of them.

First, let me bluntly ask you a very serious question. Do you want to be an actor who works their whole life? Do you want to be an artist who not only acts, but can also do many other creative things throughout their career? Do you want to be famous? Do you want to be famous fast with very little work or study or practice or any auditioning at all? This book can help with the first two 'wants' only. This is not an "I can make you famous!" book. Unfortunately I still get questions from potential students who want me to teach them how to be 'famous'. I see young 'actors' who do not know who Tennessee Williams is, have never seen a black and white movie, do not enunciate, have never read a play, have never read a film script and do not even care to – they just want attention or fame. As the internet takes over more of our lives, I encounter more and more young people who say they want to 'act', but really they just seem to want fame and the fastest, easiest and laziest route to get to it. They want to be noticed. Today that is quite easy to do. Post naked selfies, run around online and be wacky. That gets you momentary fame, some celebrity, and that may indeed be what you desire. But – this book is not meant for those people. Granted there is at least one exception to every rule, so it is very possible that the laziest, non-actor in the world will be hired (perhaps because they are gorgeous) for a TV series or movie. However, I guarantee you they will not have a long and productive career and will not be respected by their peers. They will not win that very special acting award and get to make that very special speech.

This book is for the artists and actors and educators who understand that this is truly a craft, who want to be better at it, especially with new technologies entering the acting world, who want to have more information, who want to work harder and be the very best at their craft, particularly now, when the industry is changing so rapidly. Would you build a cabinet with absolutely no tools and training? Nope. Neither should you enter the craft of acting without having good tools and training.

There has *never* been a better and easier time in history for a younger or older, gay or straight, black, Asian, Hispanic, female, trans or even just an average white actor to be proactive about their career, their contacts, their tools of representation, and how and when they meet and network with those who can help them move further in their careers. There has never been a more exciting time to work with new and developing technology in the various entertainment fields. Since you are going to be constantly competing against many other very motivated and knowledgeable people, you must make a plan and be very proactive about making it work. This book can help.

Artists called in for a motion capture audition who have no idea what that is will probably not get the work. You may fall into an initial voice over audition accidently, perhaps because you may have an interesting voice, but you will not make a career of it unless you train and prepare solidly. You may go into an audition feeling like you have the film role 'nailed' but then you have no idea what to do when the director tells you the scene should have a 'Felliniesque type feel'. Your college or training program usually, as good as it may be (and as needed for any actor), will not prepare you for the real world as an actor in many ways. You will graduate still thinking you should say 'scene' after doing an audition monologue for a casting director, and you may have never been on an actual film set or auditioned for a regional theater.

John Bell, founder of The Bell Shakespeare Company in Australia, regards formal acting training as a necessary rite of passage: "You don't want to be teaching actors as you are directing, it just doesn't seem fair."

You may graduate from a training program knowing that you are a well rounded artist, but you have never once been on camera, you do not have a headshot and you may have no idea what a slate is. These are the basics for actors – they don't even approach dealing with the amazing (and sometimes frustrating!) new technologies such as a blue screen audition or the digital transfer of reels and headshots.

This book comes from seventeen seasons running a theater company in New York City, working with many of the best actors around the world, many other years as a working actor in film and theater in both Los Angeles and New York City, years spent in rehearsal rooms and on TV and film sets, many additional times casting shows and/or assisting in casting for television, voice work, film and stage. Combine all that with my own lecturing and teaching over the past ten years and I am lucky enough to have mapped the vast changes over the past fifteen years, both as an actor and as a casting person/producer and director. I am more than computer and technical program savvy as well, and so should you be if you want to be an actor in this digital and rapidly changing online landscape.

The growing trends in digital media, film and the internet are shaping daily how we work, audition, write, cast, film and create art. The changing trends in reality TV and foreign TV now shape what casting directors search for in the United States. Current trends that will only continue (and for which many actors are unprepared) include greatly increased self taping, much more diverse casting, roles written specifically for the LGBTQIA community and for the disabled artist, casting foreign actors in the United States and casting American actors overseas, a more expansive and greater variety of work for voice actors (and many more ways to get your foot in that door), much more motion capture, blue and green screen film work, more actors needed with multiple languages and more accent roles available for actors who can do the accents, and – believe it or not – much more ability to find and book fairly substantial amount of TV, film and stage work without needing an agent or manager as you begin. With an additional threat in late 2017 of the end of 'net neutrality', you need to be fully in the loop as to what this all could mean for your career, your future, and your control of it. Being able to chart these future trends and learning from past and current trends are the best ways an actor can prepare for this coming century of work.

1

HOW TO USE THIS BOOK
AND WHY NOW?

Don't do anything out of weakness or desperation.
James Morrison, working actor, musician and father

There are about a million books about acting and auditioning on the market. Well, at least maybe some hundreds. Why should you read this one? Why does it matter right now? The entertainment industry has been going through huge and startling changes within the past twenty years and many artists are not paying attention. Everything from advertising to auditioning and casting to marketing and distribution, filming and editing has changed – not to mention the globalization and internationalization of all types of entertainment via the internet. Now, with the war over net neutrality looming, this will impact entertainment and how actors in the arts book jobs and create their work online.

China, interestingly enough, is now actually the world's biggest film market, nearly $250 million greater globally than the US in 2017. Add into that market mix the overwhelming and as yet undiscussed impact of reality TV on both theater and film. In addition, original content providers such as Amazon, Netflix and Hulu are raking in huge funds and producing more and more new (and sometimes actor created) content, and may very well jump to adding in augmented reality (AR), virtual reality (VR) or 360 video (both of which are explained in the glossary) in order to keep their new audiences attentive and loyal. Lastly, add in a heap of new media, new production possibilities and new streaming, web, audio and video opportunities, and you have quite a vastly different field for actors and other artists from what it was twenty years back. Are you able to compete as an actor in this new digital world?

There are tons of books written about how to audition and how to act, but many fewer about what not to do, how to work in newer media (blue screen, voice work, anime dubbing and motion capture), what you do in auditions that can cost you the job and how to capitalize on some of the growing technology trends, as well as how to prepare and rehearse at home for things you will encounter in this new world of entertainment. As well, it helps to have a great deal of the above information all in one book geared toward current trends and taxes; internet, online casting platforms; and new and emerging technologies that you could very well work into your career.

There are so many questions actors have about new technologies and many they do not even know they have until they blow an audition or a contracted job on a set – this book is intended to answer as many of them as possible. Some answers, many in fact, are technology based and many are simply things you wish someone had told you that you needed to do or were doing wrong in an audition. There will also be various exercises that you can do at home and a few technical references throughout this book.

Really though, if you think about it, what has technology and globalized digital access done to change the industry of film and stage? There are the obvious changes: blue and green screen development and the growing market for computer generated imagery (CGI) and motion capture, more globalization and greater ability to create and market materials or even your own career online, as well as how reality TV has changed the casting and "look" of both TV and film. Stage as well has become much more technology friendly, incorporating holograms and multimedia, puppets, and audio and video aspects to a degree never seen before in theater. There are even stage production companies now creating and marketing film trailers for their staged theater productions. Yep, film trailers for stage productions. Books and audiobooks now have film trailers as well. Books! That is the way they can stay competitive in this changing market.

Tools of the Trade: The World of APPS

So, in this ever changing landscape of entertainment what tools of the trade does every actor have to have in order to work in this digital age? Well, unlike ten or fifteen years ago now there are actually computer and phone applications (apps) which can assist you in your career, one of which is called Rehearsal. It is a line learning app but it also can record lines and scenes and can be used to submit those recorded files for voice auditions. Each of the main acting unions has an app now to see auditions and pay dues, as do the casting platforms actorsaccess.com, *Backstage* and other websites and IMDb. There are apps for acting quizzes, acting practice, auditions, scene study and more. Some of these apps are Castivate, Offbook, Scenebot, AuditionCal, Scenestudy, IMDb, iPerform, and ActorGenie. You will find out more about them in the resources section of this book. These apps are but a few of the new tools you may need. If you have a phone that works with apps and do not have a few of these on it that is the first thing you need to look at and then download what works for you. What other apps do you need? If you are union there is one set, and another set if you are not. Look at them all carefully and get your phone and computer setup. This is vital. Which apps do I recommend? Any and all, what works for you is what you need. However, do learn your lines old school way, by running them yourself. Then if you do drop your phone and break it you are not dependent upon it for your lines. Learn to work with technology, but do not become dependent upon it and let it make you a lazy actor.

Twenty years ago the whole world of 'apps' did not even exist. Twenty years ago the technical requirements for young actors at auditions were very different compared to now. You had an 8 × 10 hard copy picture or two and your resume (trimmed to be 8 × 10 as well) was stapled to the back of it. Perhaps if you were really cool back then you had a composite card (a 4 × 6 heavy paper card with three to four pictures of yourself) or a few clips of yourself acting (all subtitled with the program you were in and the episode number) and all edited together on a clunky VHS cassette tape. This was called your reel.

Tools of the Trade: Digital Everything

Now in 2018 you must have the same kinds of pictures and resumes, but really only a few hard copies (as little as ten per year), as most of your submissions will be digital via email, your agent or a casting website. (Also, know the correct digital size to send, please. If I get a digital headshot that is huge and not easy to see the minute I click on it, then I will not scroll down and sideways to see it – I will delete it.) You also must have an acting reel (or even two) around two minutes long, with anywhere from six to fifteen clips of yourself acting, but you do not need to subtitle any of the clips currently in 2018. Why? Because there are so many types of media online and offline now and nine million cable stations and web series and international TV channels that it is harder to track all of them and subtitling has fallen by the wayside (which is a great thing for new actors as you can now create and film your own clips if you are starting out).

Now in 2018 a smart actor also not only carries a cell phone, but has the ability to carry headshots, reels and video clips of your work as links in that cell phone. Then that smart actor can text or email anyone their info, links and pics anywhere, anytime. You want to be the smart young actor that when a casting person says, "Yes, please send me your headshot, reels and resume," you do it right there and then on the spot and they see it then and there and remember you. Do not be the actor who sends it all two weeks later and they have no idea who you are or why you sent it.

Now in 2018 actors can text agents, casting people, movie stars and even email them all as well. Regarding texting, however, just because you can text does not mean that you should. If you cannot spell well, please do not text or email casting people. A spellcheck is in every computer, phone, iPad and so forth. Use them. If you are not well spoken and have a limited vocabulary get an app that is a word a day dictionary and learn a word a day. Make certain that you have a dictionary app on your phone. Actors deal with words every moment of their career – they are storytellers – and if you cannot read a scene without fumbling for pronunciation (or, worse yet, if you assume you will be told how to say the words in the audition) or write an email without seventeen spelling and grammatical errors then you must work doubly hard. You must be able to come in and cold read anything and everything without missing a beat, and if you have had the scene a week to practise it and still mispronounce words we know you have not worked on it and you probably will not be cast. If you cannot read the words how can you memorize them and how can we have confidence in your acting them?

New Tools for the 21st Century

There are now many additional tools actors must have in the 21st century. As mentioned, you do not have to subtitle which television show the clips in your reel are from, leaving open many media possibilities that you can create, write and film yourself. YouTube clips and self written, self taped clips are now accepted so long as they look well done and are lit well. So, you then get a reel and picture and resume and you are done, right? No, you now need so much more. Two reels at the minimum are best eventually (dramatic and comedy), as well as an actor website.

Should stage actors have acting reels? Yes, absolutely. If you are an actor of any kind in this digital age, you should have at least one reel and many stage and film actors have two or more. If you only do stage work, you still need a reel with clips of you on stage in shows that can be put on that actor website you need to have online, as well as on any casting websites. In 2017 even stage plays themselves began to develop trailers, video trailers, to interest potential audience members. Large regional theaters and NY theaters have special agreements with unions to be able to record promotional segments of their actors for TV and websites. My own company was given a special agreement by the Actor's Equity Association for a film crew to follow our production all the way from casting to performance in 2014–2015 in order to film the documentary, *Two and Twenty Troubles*.

Your own YouTube channel is also a tool of great benefit, and you can have at least one voice over reel, membership in Actors Access or *Backstage* (although I have a few issues with *Backstage* and the new Clapit app they encourage, which I will discuss in a bit) and eventually a page on IMDb, interlinks of everything to everything else, and activity on social media of all kinds – Facebook, Twitter, Instagram, MySpace, etc. Also, please have a valid passport (and note that on your resume as international casting has risen in huge numbers in the past fifteen years) and have all necessary forms of identification. You do not want to get cast and have no social security card or valid work permit.

What kinds of parts are being written in the 21st century and how can you find and book those new roles? Compared with ten or fifteen years ago there are now far more leading female roles (still not enough though to be equitable), LGBTQIA roles (and I mean roles written from the start for LGBTQIA actors, not ones changed under pressure from straight roles to gay roles in order to have a token gay character) and roles written for people of color (and with the enormous and well-deserved recent success of *Black Panther*, this is sure now to increase). There are a lot more roles written that are realistic, gritty and natural, and that say things we all may think but do not say in polite society. Shows such as *Girls*, *Orange is the New Black* and *Transparent* are written specifically not only to be honest and real, but to put reality out there and into the faces of the viewing public. They are written to challenge viewing audiences. This is very different from the politically correct, mostly white, non-disabled and all gorgeous and model-y heterosexual people TV shows of the past.

Agents and Managers

What about agents and managers in the 21st century? Many actors are not even sure of the difference between agents and managers, and there is a big difference. Agents are federally regulated and can only take (at the top amount) 20 percent commission on your work (in the United Kingdom this can be as high as 25 percent for modeling commissions). Many actors also do not know that in film and TV casting whatever casting company hires you most usually directly pays your agent their 15 or 20 percent commission in addition to paying you your fee as an actor. It is a rare situation where an actor writes their agent a commission check directly. In theater this can be much more flexible and agents and actors may work out a variety of ways to be certain all get paid. An agent (especially one who is franchised by the unions, meaning that agent has to adhere to union rules whether or not the job or you are union) is primarily concerned with getting you work, getting you auditions and contracts and jobs. That is usually about it for their job description. If you have an agent who likes you and helps you with other things (getting you into a great commercial class or recommending a coach), so much the better.

A manager, however, is not federally regulated (nor are they union franchised), so they can ask any commission they want and most importantly that commission comes out of your pocket, nobody else's. A manager can also try to get you auditions, and they really do need to be very well connected, but another thing they really can do is to manage your public persona, your celebrity, keeping you in the public eye. A manager has also got to have an incredible pedigree in that they know people, all the right people, to help your career. If you sign with a manager without doing an online check for their social media, contacts and appearances in articles and at events, you are doing it wrong. They *must* know people. Managers often can be the key to getting work for a child actor, as very early on children need contacts. A manager, if you become known, may even have their staff take over all your social media for your fans once you become 'hot'. Publicists used to do a lot of this twenty years ago but now managers and publicists sometimes overlap in their work.

When do you need an agent? If you are getting work, making some money and even joining a union you are not necessarily in dire need of an agent, as you are already booking work. If you have done a few off-Broadway shows, a few roles on a TV show and are moving up, then you would do well to have one. You do not need one fresh out of college and it is often better if you take a few years and build a resume before you approach anyone about representation. Of course there are exceptions to every rule, but in order to be ready to have an agent you must habitually be punctual, be professional, have a very good resume and be very good at auditioning. All this *before* you get that agent.

When do you need a manager? When you are on the verge of a big award nomination, when you begin to get approached on the street for autographs, when you cannot manage your online fan base, when you really are ready to be 'managed' by being told what to wear to the Emmys and where to go to be seen, then you may be ready for a manager. You do not, however, need one and many actors have agents and no managers. A manager can also act as an agent and get you seen for auditions, but their main job usually is to manage where you are seen and make sure your face is kept in the public eye. A manager is the one who, when you have lunch with an old high school buddy, arranges for the paparazzi to 'accidentally' catch you having a secret lunch so that those pics can go on the news outlets and keep your name in the public eye.

Once you do have a meeting with an agent, do not be so over-whelmed and excited to meet them that you ask no questions at all and sign whatever papers they offer you. Any audition, interview or meet of any kind is always a two way street. Be aware of this and ask a few of the following questions:

(A) About the Agent and Agency Itself:

1. In which areas are they interested in representing you? (TV, film, new media, modeling, voice over, singing, international work, commercials, stage work?)
2. If you eventually need a manager do they have managers on staff?
3. How long is the freelance agreement if freelancing (freelancing being exactly the same as being signed with them, except you do not actually sign a contract), and how long is the contract for if not freelancing, but actually signing?
4. What is their commission on your work? In the bigger markets like New York and Los Angeles it may be 10–15 percent. In smaller markets where there may be only one or two agents their commission is usually 20 percent. If an agent asks for more than that they are not a real agent, they are a scam. Agents are federally monitored and cannot ask for more than 20 percent.
5. How should you keep in touch with the agent? Phone? Email? Text? This is vital as these days there are cell phones, BlackBerrys (yes, still), landlines, emails, texts, faxes, instant messaging and so on. If your agent is texting you and you are a phone person then you will miss that text and the audition. Be sure you know not only how to contact your agent and how they can contact you, but also how often that contact should happen. Should you call in daily? Weekly? Text them every three days?
6. Ask the agent what do they feel the agency is known for? Exciting new talent? Reliable character actors? Diversity and inclusion? If you are a young black actor you do not necessarily want to be at an agency with character actors who are over sixty and white. The agent works for you, so make sure they are the right one.

(B) About the Contracts and You

1. What geographical area does the contract cover? Is it only your state, your city, a tri-state area? Does it cover an international

market as well? Do they have a sister office in New York City, Los Angeles, London, Ontario?

2. How does the agent see you? What interested them in you?

3. What roles can they see submitting you for? Listen very closely to this answer. You do not want to be boxed into 'dumb blonde' or anything else. Actors of color and actors with disabilities do not want to hear stereotypes in this answer at all.

4. What age range do they see you playing? It should be a solid five or ten year age range that you can do, 20–30, or 18–28, or 40–50. If you are 25 and they see submitting you for 45 year olds, then something is off.

5. Any actor/actress of color needs to be asking what roles an agent would submit you for – for certain? Do not let yourself be put into a stereotyped box of casting because of your color. Black and Hispanic actors should not be constantly auditioning for maids; Arabic actors should not be constantly reading for terrorists; the same for disabled artists. You want them talking about submitting you for roles with and without disability. Disability and color are non issues in this changing world and you want an agent who sees everything in you. Demand the best from them before you sign.

6. Can you still promote or submit yourself for things? They may ask you not to submit for auditions and to only let them submit you for work. If you submit yourself for something, not your agent, and you get the job you still need to know if they still get a commission. They may tell you to keep it, or they may ask that they still get the commission though they did not submit you for the part. Perhaps they will use that part to tell everyone about it and get you cast in more things. All the options are fine, but you need to know all of this before you sign anything.

(C) What to Look for While You Wait in the Lobby of the Agent's Office. Pay Attention

1. Is it a busy office with a lot of people working? Or are there two employees bored to death? A boring office is not one you want working for you. You want an office where phones are ringing and contracts are being signed.

2.   Is it clean, are there pictures of artists they represent on the walls? If the office is not clean and they do not post their actors' pictures then they are, again, not working for you. A dirty office space means they do not take their work seriously and they will not take your work seriously either.

3.   Are pictures of their talent diverse in color and age or do they all look like you? If they all are your age, race and type then not only are you competing for roles, but you are competing within your own agent's talent roster. If that does not bother you, great, but know then they think of you as one of many, not one of a kind.

4.   Are they telling you that you need new headshots, resumes, dance lessons, acting lessons, etc. and that you should only go to whom they tell you to get these things? And that conveniently all those things are in their building with their staff? STOP. *This is a scam.* If you truly need new headshots they will tell you and you will be responsible for getting them done, or they may even pay or split the cost. Just do not walk into an 'agency' and pay out any money. Ever. EVER. I cannot stress this enough.

Do not ever ask an agent, or an acting coach for that matter, how many clients do you have? Have you made anyone a star? Whom can you introduce me to? This will kill any conversation, and you should always be aware that you are building both a resume and a reputation. Questions like this are about 'fame', and not about being an actor. However, asking the other questions listed above will ensure you sign with the right agent for you and that they also know they are signing a smart actor. Good agents never have issues with you asking them smart questions. They prefer smart actors. If you begin asking these questions and are met with anger from an agent, get up and leave. A real agent will love that you ask questions, a scammer will not.

Scams and How To Spot Them

Beware and beware again of the numerous scams masquerading as agents or talent groups. You read about them all the time. The big tip off is that they promise you work and fame. These are agencies that are not real agencies; they put on the big regional 'talent conferences' where you supposedly meet many agents and managers. You 'get accepted' into many categories (each one with a separate entry fee) and memorize whatever they give you. What mostly happens is you spend a lot of money to meet people and do monologues for them and that is it. Any time you pay $2,000 for training that lasts one day, or $8,000 because your kiddo got into the 'super duper' session of such and such a program, *stop*. This is a scam.

Do your research and look the company or organization up online, check ripoffreport.com and the Better Business Bureau. Many times I will get asked about agencies that are scams and all you have to do is check them online. Use the internet. Spend your money on a real acting or audition coach; spend your money to get voice over training or stunt work and not on scam artists or conventions or gatherings that go nowhere. California and New York have strict labor laws for child performers, both on and off set, but parents must also be on guard, especially when their child is non union, at these week long 'talent' events that go on for hours.

Child Actors in the New Age

Scams and how they work lead me to how any of this book pertains to young actors under eighteen. Actors under eighteen always come with parents. There are parents and then there are stage parents. Stage parents usually are in charge of what the child is involved in, not the child (and yes children should always have a say in what they audition for once they get to be about nine or so), and exhibit one of two behaviors. Coddlers seem to live through their child, limiting them to sweet monologues, often taken directly from TV or film and memorized exactly, with the same emphasis and breath, as the original scene. They limit their child to innocent roles that they choose, and often you find that their child has little or no interest in acting at all. It is excruciating to watch a child who hates performing being forced to do it. Parents of children need to understand that if a child is pushed into acting we know it. We see it in the audition tape and in person. Chances are the child will not be cast because we see the misery he/she is in. The other route parents take is to become the second kind of stage parents.

My mother allowed me to be cast in a horror film without reading the script. It was the worst horror film ever made. It was about cannibal children who all get murdered at the end. So there I was, doing my first movie and getting stabbed in the back by an extra they decided would be my mother.

Akin Salawu

Stage parents of potential child actors are by far the biggest market for scam agencies because they capitalize on the parents' obsession to make their child famous. This second type of parents are easily bilked of funds and often are both parents and managers of their child and thus believe they know how to direct their child, manage their child, represent their child, coach their child, well you get the idea. They frequently will push their children into more demanding roles, older roles, without seeing if the child is uncomfortable with it or if the work is a scam. They will make unreasonable demands to directors or casting people and often cost their children a job due to those demands. Neither of these types of parents seem to realize that they do cost their child work, and neither of these types of parents ever seems truly interested in whether their child enjoys acting and auditioning at all.

I've been really lucky when it comes to casting kids, and I don't particularly like child actors. Too often, they just show up, and they've had whatever real innocence that's in a child just beaten out of them. They start to perform for you, and you can just see it coming. It's no good.

Jeff Nichols, casting staff

Another thing that costs children work is when they are not allowed to be children in real life – when every moment of their life is in an audition or acting or singing or dancing class, when they have no free time to have friends and just be kids. I, as a casting director, do not want to meet little adults when I cast children. I want to see and cast real children. Let your children be children, how else can they perform like a child? Dakota Fanning is an example of a very talented young child who, even though she had the ability to access and act with real nearly adult levels of emotion, was still a child. Not a small adult. Let kids be kids. That is what we look for when we audition them.

One should also, parents, always be aware of the reality on the casting side, the agent's side, as I am when I cast kids. I always realize that not only am I casting that kid, but I am also casting the parents. I will not cast a child whom I see is uncomfortable or who does not love acting. Ever. The parent is as important as the child though, as they will be in rehearsal and performance and on the set at all times. If the parent is annoying, high maintenance, overbearing, etc., then that is what you get to deal with, as does your whole cast and crew. If you have an extremely obnoxious parent, you may end up not casting the child even if they are the most talented one. This is how a few very talented young actors constantly lose roles, because their parents are pushy and overbearing and make it about themselves. The parents push so much that, even though the child is very talented (and may even love acting), the prospect of dealing with the parent is far more trouble than a casting person and director can stand. The parents, in these cases, want the fame and attention for themselves, not for their children, and they cost their children work. Often is it not until their children are over eighteen (and have more control over their careers) that they begin to book work.

A question I ask my students at times is, do you want to be an actor who works, or be famous? Revealing yourself online is not fame; it brings only momentary interest and the internet lives forever, it will not forget the topless shots you posted online. Reality shows are also not a career, although they can get you momentary interest and money. Nobody, nobody really can make you famous. If you do not train, do not understand reading, do not audition, then it is highly unlikely that you will get famous as an actor. If you do not know the basics you will truly find it hard to get work. An audition is not the place to be taught how to act, pronounce words or how to audition.

What has not changed about acting for stage or film in the past twenty years? Truth, honesty, persona, reputation, being 'live' and real. Connecting. Acting is about words and reading – if you do not like words, talking (or signing if you are deaf), and reading, please do not become an actor. Learn not only to read, but to read aloud or sign. Gain a vocabulary and learn not one, but two new words a day.

If you cannot read a scene or monologue, if you think it is cool to be monosyllabic and say, "uh . . ." all the time, you will most likely not get cast. Truly.

The myth of being discovered with no experience may indeed happen once in a million years, but what happens after that? The young actor to be 'discovered' is then sent to coaches, speech teachers, groomers, stylists and more who prep them heavily for the set. If you are so gorgeous that people fall over or if you are related to someone famous who helps you this may happen for you, but if not then you *must* work.

A few of the exercises that follow in this book may make you say, "Well, heck that is simple, I get it. Why should I practise?" Because those who book the jobs practise, they work out their improvisation muscles, they know how to nail a look to the camera. They know how to button a scene. They know how much to move when they are in a close-up versus when they are framed at the hips. They nail that high C in their Broadway musical audition. They cold read like a dream and do voice over auditions that shine. They understand a blue screen audition and commit to it. They practise, they audition like a professional and they earn it. You will be competing against them and you need to be ready.

2

ACTING FOR FILM AND THE VARIATIONS OF FILM

I had a moment of inspiration and I went with it. I trusted myself
and I booked the gig.

> Henry Winkler, 1983 lecturer at Cal-arts (speaking in
> reference to being told to comb his hair in the mirror
> at a callback and instead going, "Aayy!" Like he was
> too perfect to touch his hair. This became an iconic
> film clip for the TV series *Happy Days*.)

How is film acting and casting for it different from how it was fifteen
years ago? Although I am loath to admit it, reality TV for all its bad
qualities has actually impacted the TV casting world in a positive way,
in that casting directors are now much more likely to cast 'regular
looking' actors, older actors, actors of color, disabled and LGBTQIA
actors. Present day TV audiences now really enjoy seeing people who
look more like them than ever before in history. Gone are the days
of glamour shots and heavy makeup; now it is the natural and real
look for both men and women on TV and that is a plus. Variety in
height and weight and skin color and disability is also a welcome
change due to shifting societal values and the full globalization of
entertainment. Our definition of true beauty is changing as well.

A factor that matters less now than ten or fifteen years ago is what
market or regional area you are an actor in. With self-taping and
smaller regional markets (like Atlanta or Albuquerque) becoming hubs
for a great deal of work, you do not now need to be an hour from
New York or Los Angeles to find work as an actor. You do need to
know the local market of your city and state, though. Who is who?

What are the biggest casting agencies, agents, film studios, recording studios, theater companies, film schools with student filmmakers in your town? Even in small towns in Ohio there is a local talent market and you should know what it is to market yourself to work in it. Information about this also lets you know if there is a tiny local market and you have to expand your auditions to the next county. Every new student of mine and I always do a solid look at their local market. A great way to know who is doing what, and where, is to check your state film commission website, which will give you a lot of information about film and TV shooting in your area. Take note of who is casting for those shows and start by sending your resume and picture there. Add local casting agents, directors and film companies on Facebook and your social media and you will start to be in the loop locally.

There are also many more types of deliberately different roles (female leads, LGBTQIA characters, disabled roles) being written these days, with the result being that casting directors, writers and directors of film are searching for much more variety not only in types of actors, but even in the range a single actor can play. If you, as an actor, have 'typecast' yourself as the good guy, or the surfer dude, I urge you to now move way beyond that. You are a blank slate and the best actors (the ones who work consistently) can put any kind of role onto that slate and embody it. You have more chances of getting cast the more you have a range and do not limit yourself. For example, there is a small minority of actors (mostly male, although there are a few females) who will not audition for or play gay roles, ever. This is absolutely fine; however, it is a way in which you limit your talent, your castability and your career. Again, it is a very personal choice – just know that each and every personal choice you make also impacts how you are defined as an actor and how much you can and will be cast. If you are biracial but only wish to audition for one of those races you again have made a choice that limits you in how you can be cast. Make these choices carefully. Give yourself every opportunity, as there are enough people out there who will limit you. Do not limit yourself.

Mostly, and I hate still having to say this to young actors, look like your darn pictures. If you have a scar or a crooked ear, be proud of it and let it show. I have actually seen actors (women mostly) not get cast because they look nothing like their pictures. Perhaps they spent a fortune on picture day and had their hair and makeup professionally done. Mistake. Unless you have that hair and makeup person live at your house and they can make you look like that every single day, do not do it. Look like you, the normal you on a really good day. With the advances in iPhones, more and more actors are able to actually take their own basic headshots, crop and lighten or edit them, put their name on them and use them as very basic shots at least until they make enough money to afford a headshot session with a good photographer. I have seen many iPhone shots where you cannot tell the difference between that and a studio shot. Many actresses are doing headshots now with no makeup at all, and they are gorgeous and natural. Often these iPhone or makeup-less shots are wonderful because it really looks like the actor at their natural best, not like a heavily altered studio shoot. However, no matter how you take the shot, be sure your finished product looks professional or it will cost you work. A few great photographers are in the resources section.

Film Resumes for the Current Market

What should be on a film resume now that was not needed twenty years ago? Twenty years ago you were an actor 'only' and most of what was on your resume focused only on that. Now in the 21st century you may be an actor/stuntman, or an actor/model, or an actress/voice over actor. All of this is fine and now shows off on your resume. I remember as a young actor and singer being told to make singing a separate resume many times. Now, you do not have to unless you want to have a specific singing career focus. To date I have an acting resume, a voice over resume, a directing resume, a fight directing resume and an accent coach resume. However, I also have a multi-purpose one with the best credits from all of the above on it and that works well too. A great tip is to put film credits first on a film resume and theater credits first on a theater resume and so forth.

Diversity is not only a word that can apply to various groups – it actually applies to what you may have on a resume now. Any and all accents (that you do perfectly) and languages you speak with at least a semi-fluent level should always be on a resume now as international casting is growing by the week. State clearly that you have a valid passport. State that you do things not many people do anymore, like drive a stick shift or ride a horse or ice skate. I know two young actors who got their SAG cards because they could drive a stick shift! There are new things that were not around commonly fifteen years ago, but which you should now note. Wire work is one, blue screen work is one, multiple foreign accents are another. A last note – keep the resume to one page. It must be attachable to the back of your headshot and one page is all we need. Even digital resumes must be only one page. We do not read five pages of resume. I have seen resumes and pictures tossed because there is more than one page of a resume. Put your best credits on one page, digital or hard copy, and that's all.

With technology taking over American life, activities that we used to take for granted have now become special skills on an acting resume. This is now a technology oriented age, so 'older' things like roller skating, pogo stick riding, horseback riding, even throwing a frisbee well, are not things everyone does now. So if you do them well make sure we know about it. Do not, by the way, put on your resume under special skills, "I am good with children and pets, know word and excel, can troubleshoot computers." You are an actor, not a nanny or IT person. At callbacks we will see if you get along with kids when you read the scene with them, or we will ask you about your computer knowledge if it pertains to the role. Note your acting and performance skills and so forth only (and I include in that choir, tech skills and so forth as well). In addition, check the phone number and messaging issue in the next chapter for theater resumes as it is true for any current resume in 2018.

Commercials and Social Media

Social media and you. It sounds like a commercial title, but I cannot say enough about the power of social media in this century and even more in the future. You do not have to be on every single social media site, but you should at minimum have an actor website, an IMDb page as soon as you can, a Facebook profile and be on one other site (Twitter, Instagram or whatever is a large online site). This is now vital for actors.

There are a variety of social media platforms and the three that seem to be the most productive for young actors are Instagram, Twitter and Facebook. Many actors even have 'actor' accounts on these and then their separate personal accounts under a nickname. Actor accounts are used to publicize jobs you get, and for people you meet, work you do. Do not post bikini shots, on set shots of scripts or privileged information, or anything about who you do not like or a bad audition you had. Your actor life on social platforms is positive, strong and all about your talent, humility, humor and work ethic. Well managed social media can even get you cast, as shown by Bria Vinaite who was cast in a lead role in *The Florida Project* from her Instagram account.

Commercial auditions as well have been directly impacted by reality TV and social media in that now dialogue, even for commercials, is much more reality based, appears off the cuff, and often is taken from improvised scenarios. You may even find yourself auditioning for commercials with no script in your hand at all or being asked to continue talking after the scripted dialogue ends. Thinking on your feet is key to booking commercial work. At heart there are really five types of commercials: sales, food, product, testimonial or spokesperson and non-dialogue commercials. We will cover all of them in this book.

What does social media have to do with acting and booking film or TV jobs? Recently a *Game of Thrones* actress commented that she was cast in her role over another young British actress because she had a larger social media following. She was not kidding, at all. I cannot tell you how many times, when deciding between the final two or three actors, a film director now goes online and looks them all up and more often than not casts the one with the largest social media following. I detest this, I really do, but it is the truth and is a trend I only see getting bigger, especially with younger directors who are much more social media aware. If you have a big following then the assumption is that you will have a built in audience. Networking is the name of the game and if you are not actively on social media and being connected to others it will hamper you in the long run in being cast.

The correct career choices are also more important now than in the past. How often should your reel be up to date and what should be on it? (Again, very different from twenty years ago when a reel was not even needed a lot of the time.) Some actors may have a dramatic reel, a comedy reel, a stand-up comedy reel, a reel of them doing accents – it all depends on you and your agent or how you want to market yourself. On an actor website you have the room to put all of your reels and show them off. Have as many as you need. The simple fact is that an actor can also have more control over their career right now than ever before. However you have to understand what the playing field is and what the game is on that field before you can play it well.

One very simple thing that very few actors pay attention to is their face and body. Knowing your face and body can also help you choose reel clips and present your reels better. Now I am not telling you to lose weight or get a nose job. You just need to know what you are working with as an actor, understand it and then use it. So, a few simple exercises.

Exercise 1: Learn Your Face

Get a blank sheet of paper and stand facing your bathroom mirror.

Note that I am not asking you to act in the mirror, as this is not ever something you want to do. Just look at your face. Now cover half of your face lengthwise and study the half that you can see. Look at the eyebrows, the cheekbones, the ear, the line of the jaw. Spend some good time studying this side of your face – how does it make you feel? What kind of person do you see? Is it a soft face? Hard? A hero? A criminal? What do you see, what do you feel? Then after a few minutes change sides and study the other side of your face. Do the same exercise. Why? You need to understand both sides of your face so you know how to work with a camera. The sides of our face are very different (sometimes drastically so) and if you have a hero side and a villain side you had better know it, so you can play the camera in an audition. The camera sees what you let it see, so you need to know your face.

Actors may often complain about models often being cast in roles. However if there is one type of person who knows the sides, planes and angles of their face it is a model. They may not be an actor, but gosh they look good. Make sure, for film work, that you understand the planes, bones, lights and shadows of your face as well as a model does. Do your best to understand what your face looks like at every single angle. What angle is your most dangerous or evil? What angles are your most angelic? If you read a scene and hold the correct side of your face to the camera I am 60 percent more likely to cast you. I have literally seen wonderful actors not get cast for an, 'I just can't put my finger on it', reason. The reason was that the actor had the wrong side of their face to the camera and that angelic look talked them right out of playing the tough cop, even though they were the best actor.

Exercise 2: All About the Eyes

Let's try a second exercise with your eyes and three very strong emotions. Still looking in your bathroom mirror cover up the bottom half of your face with that piece of paper. Relax your forehead and keep it smooth. Now look into your own eyes, as film is really all about the eyes, and think of whatever makes you see a change in your own eyes. What image, feeling or sound or memory makes you angry? Someone kicking a kitty? I mean *real* rage, not ticked off. You need to be able to find what makes rage shine in your eyes. Once you do have a trigger (a thought, a person, a smell, an image) and once you confirm that it works you can then use that on a set or in an audition. Try this exercise with rage, laughter and sadness and see what you get. Find the trigger and see it in your own eyes. These triggers are tools. Emotional triggers are just more tools to go into your actor bag when you travel to auditions or when you are on the set or stage.

While many of the exercises in this book are great to do in the mirror for your own focus on a camera spot, or to see something I am asking you to look for, be careful not to act into the mirror or act for the mirror or for yourself. Watching your own face and altering your behavior or look after watching yourself is not what you want to do. Acting is what happens inside you and in combination with the text and director, not about what happens on your face. If acting moments are real and true there is no way we or the camera cares what your face looks like. Acting happens inside, not in the mirror.

While you can get away with a much more relaxed type of conversational speech in film and TV (not commercials) than you can with stage work, that does not mean that you should be monosyllabic and have no diction. It does not mean that you can have a very small vocabulary. If I am in a filmed scene where I whisper dramatic things then I had better be able to be heard because I have good diction. For film you can be more relaxed, yes, but if you audition and we cannot understand the scene when we play it back later, then you will not get cast. Make sure you are not your worst enemy. Help us to cast you.

3

ACTING FOR STAGE AND MUSICALS: THE BASICS

Even if you aren't the prettiest girl in the room, you can always make room for yourself if you have talent. There is not a limited number of spaces, there is always room for you.

Judith Ivey, 1983 lecturer at Cal-arts

How is stage acting and musical theatre, and casting for them, different from how it was twenty years ago? Stage plays are now being written with much more relevant and realistic plots and increasingly diverse casts (more roles for people of color and women as well as for older actors and disabled artists), while stage is adding in more technical elements (multimedia, video, the cast doing puppetry or playing musical instruments) than ever before in theater history. The genres of songs are also becoming much more diverse. We now have country-western musicals, we have *Hamilton* and hip-hop, we have jazz and rock.

In my audition for *South Pacific*, I couldn't seem to understand what the director wanted me to do. He kept saying, "Make it bigger. Make it stronger. More force." I must have read the scene seven times before I finally asked, "Do you want it butch?" And then I ran the scene like that, they laughed, and I got the part."

Lisa Howard, actress

Theater Resumes in the Current Market

Actor resumes in this age for theater and film are very different as well. Ten or fifteen years ago you had a service or message machine listed on your resume and nothing else; you gave out no personal contact information. Personal numbers were private. Now it is very common to give an email or two, your cell phone number for texts and a message or agent number. While it is the norm, I recommend you err on the side of caution. Give out your cell number, if you must, and email, but no landline, especially for young women, that can be traced to where you live. Do not ever put your home address on a resume at all, for any reason. Unfortunately information is everywhere online and it is very easy to track where you are, so be very cautious.

Auditions in the 21st century (especially regionally and off-Broadway) are now looking for far more diverse casts, although still 65 percent of roles are for white men. There are new dos and don'ts in 21st century auditions, and many reasons for which actors do or do not get cast that are very different from those ten years ago. A good actor can even change the script or role and the entire movie with a good audition. I once sat in on an off-Broadway audition where they had wanted a middle-aged white actor for the leading role in a new play. We saw a few great actors, quite a few so-so actors and a few not so good, and then a young black actress walked in. She confessed she had talked her way into the audition by lying to the audition monitor, but that she felt that if we just gave her one shot to read the audition scene (which she had copied from her boyfriend, who had actually auditioned) we would be surprised. A slight argument went on in the room, with a few parties against it, but most of us (me included) voting on the side of hearing her. She got to read the scene and not only was amazing, but changed the project completely. As the playwright said to her, "I never understood that what this play was really about was a thirty year old black woman. Thank you," and he meant it. She got the part. The right actor can change the casting director's mind and the project completely.

Musical Auditions and How To Make Them Work

As a casting person a few of the most uncomfortable auditions I have ever seen (I do not say bad, necessarily, just very uncomfortable) have been for musicals. The actor's acting is fine, the dancing is certainly good enough for the artist to be cast, but then we get to the actual singing part of the audition and that can be where an auditionee can really lose the role. Why? The main reason is not because the artist cannot sing, but because they do not sell the song by behaving naturally when they do sing. All of a sudden we get large arm and body movements in the audition song (completely unjustified by the low emotional energy and terror of the actor) and it becomes very uncomfortable or fake and pushed. They try to act out a style of musical singing that has no root in reality. The best way around this I learned a million years ago when I auditioned for a workshop with Hal Prince. Again, if you do not know who he is, look him up (and shame on you). I was about fifteen and had begged to audition even though you had to be eighteen or older to attend the workshop. I got to audition and, of course, did not get to be in the workshop and work with Hal Prince, *but* I got invited to watch the workshop and listen and meet him. This is his favorite exercise for you, to bring life to your text in a musical audition.

Mr. Prince advised to write out your song, line by line, on one side of a piece of paper. Then write a line by line paraphrase on the other side, like so:

SONG	YOUR PARAPHRASE
Sometimes I wonder where I've been,	Some days I feel down
Who I am,	I feel lost
Do I fit in.	I am not even popular.
Make believing is hard alone,	It is hard to keep the faith.
Out here on my own. By myself.	

And so forth through the entire song. You put it into your words. This is called paraphrasing. Then take your paraphrased words and stand up, relax and read them out like a monologue to a big crowd and take note (now you can simply film yourself on your iPhone) of what your body does naturally with movement. Perhaps when you say, "I am not even popular," you find that you naturally make a fist. Note that. Any and all of the movements that you make naturally then are taken from the version with your words, and put back into the actual song so the movements in the song are not only natural but have come from your own organic impulses. Committing to doing this exercise with your audition songs will absolutely improve them and make you much more natural. Feeling more natural physically will relax you and also help your singing and the selling of the song as well.

An added note is to always make sure at any musical audition that you have a second song prepared and ready to sing, even if they do not ask for it. Much like non-singing actors who do not have a monologue in their back pocket (when asked for it) and regret it, you do not want to only have one song prepared when they ask you to do a second one. Also, always, always bring your own sheet music for anything.

> I also had an audition where the casting director had my headshot on the table. I began singing and in red marker she wrote, "NO," across my picture.
>
> Akin Salawu

You can still walk in and nail it in a musical or in any audition. You do this by being prepared and already owning that role. Quite a few years back I held auditions for *Bad Seed*, a classic dramatic tale that hinges on casting a very talented and smart eight to eleven year old girl as the evil lead. I saw many young girls and dealt with many sets of parents, a few of whom talked their child right out of the part before even auditioning ("Well, she is not union and has no experience, but we will need a weekly salary, limousine transportation to and from home and can you promise she will get an agent?"). That was just as well, as I had to not only find a brilliant child actor, but a parent or set of parents who were supportive and positive, but not in our faces during a long rehearsal process that would be demanding on the young actress. One of the last girls I saw was a ten year old who went by the name of Lee Eden at that time. She came and checked in for the audition and then asked if we had a bathroom where she could change. She changed from jeans and a t-shirt into a 1950s-feel skirt and shirt and then braided her hair. She walked out prepared and ready to kill that audition. Kill it she did, doing the very professional trick of performing the audition scene completely memorized, but with her script in hand just in case. She had done her research and had made very specific acting choices about the role and there was no doubt it was hers.

Her mother sat calmly in the lobby and was supportive of her and refreshingly low maintenance (although, truthfully, Lee was and continues to be a phenomenal young actress and singer and I would have cast her no matter what) but it was an added bonus that her mother Tanya also turned out to be a terrific human being and a great mom. This is the kind of parent who knows her child loves doing this and lets them do it. This is the kind of parent who is secure in who they are, teaches their child to also be secure in who they are and miraculously the child can then be themselves doing what they love. I cast her in that part that very day.

How are new musicals being written, cast and sung differently from fifteen years ago? A prime example of Broadway singing styles changing is the famous musical *Annie*, (originally produced in the 1970s), which was belted by everyone on stage and continued the classic Broadway belt style. For a decade after that everyone belted songs and young girls everywhere went hoarse trying to sing the title role. Now in 2017 and 2018 everything is about microphones and body mics and stage mics and an entire show being belted by every single singer is not how it is at all. Shows now are being written and cast with the full awareness that every singer will have a microphone for both dialogue acting and singing. This means that you still have to have a good voice, but you do not need to be a belter all the time anymore. You can whisper and talk and act and sing, and you can do so in an audition now too. Remember that. An actor who can act and sing at the same time is what we are on the lookout for. Do not feel you need to belt to feel real for musicals. Volume is no longer the issue. Stop belting (unless asked to) and start acting as you sing.

Digital World Impact on the Stage

How is online activity, multimedia and digital work impacting the stage in new ways now? *Dear Evan Hansen*, *The Lion King* and many other shows across the globe now employ multimedia and wire work, webcams and puppetry as a matter of fact. These things have gone from being specialty issues to the norm in theater. Performance artist Taylor Mac does full twelve hour stage shows where people are flown in across the stage and raised and lowered as a matter of course. Stage actors are now far more valuable to casting directors for learning or having worked with these technical skills, and, having worked with puppetry or multimedia on stage, it thus increases their value as performers. An additional talent that can expand your work and casting potential is more training in stage combat, with weapons such as swords, knives, and broadswords, and even some gun knowledge. If you are a male and can also work and dance in high heels (*Kinky Boots* is not the only musical that has this as a requirement) then you should note it on your resume.

What new items should be on your stage resume that were not even in the picture ten years ago? Accents you can do well and any foreign languages (international casting is the biggest it has ever been in history and US based actors with language skills are in demand), any combat (this includes military training) and gymnastics experience, weaponry (everything from guns to archery to knife throwing), any work with body or handheld mics, specialized dance (work in high heels, any and all dance styles or gymnastics), puppetry (and do specify hand puppets, marionettes, life size puppets, etc., on your resume.) and any aerial work or wire experience.

There are detractors who now say new media advances mean that film and TV will start to take over all media and so live theater is now dying. However binge-watch culture is not only happening in regard to Netflix and Hulu. The same type of viewing, once popularized by long stage plays such as *The Life and Adventures of Nicholas Nickleby*, has seen a rejuvenation and a marathon day of theater has grown once again in England, with productions such as the Donmar Warehouse's all-female Shakespeare trilogy and Chichester Festival Theatre's Chekhov season, proving British audiences are happy to watch multiple hours of drama. *Harry Potter and the Cursed Child* runs to a six hour length and already has plans to move into the US after its run in the West End of London. Once any of these shows close in London they come right to the Broadway stage in the US. This is a trend of marathon length shows that actors with talent, accents, stamina and a good background of study and performance can ride in the United States. Once these shows come to the US, they must, by union law, have a percentage of US artists. That could be you with the right study and training.

What types of daily study can benefit stage actors? Read plays, read the classics. Read about slang, new terms in language. Why? Because new plays are inspired by classics and reference them, and if you do not understand the references you will not give the best audition.

If you do not know slang you will not encounter it well in an audition. See films and plays. There are lists online: watch the 100 best films picked by critics, watch every Oscar winning film for best picture. See any plays you can locally or on tour. See musicals, comedies and dramas. Listen and learn. Constant training and watching others in your field on a daily basis teaches you to know your field, teaches you to be able to discuss your field, respect your field, understand your field and understand the references about it and thus work more in your field. Know your field. Know the people in it, know your own reputation and know how to manage it.

Knowing your field and your own reputation also helps you to respect the work and the people in the field. I once cast an actress in a large role in a United States premiere of the British play *Kosher Harry*. She rehearsed for four weeks, and although she was a bit high maintenance in rehearsals, she became close to the cast and crew and developed a wonderful role. She opened the show, did the first night of the performance and then quit because the first night, "Wasn't as fun as I thought it would be." I was forced to step in and act her role the rest of the run of fourteen shows. Had she been union I would have reported her to the union, but she was not. Once the show closed I did answer the questions brewing about why I stepped into the role, and everyone knew what her name was as this type of behavior is not only rare (why rehearse a show and then drop out after one night?) but disrespectful to everyone. She had no respect for the field, the other actors, the text, and ultimately herself. Decorum and reputation are vital, and if you blow something will people talk about it? Yes, and your name will get around as hers did.

To Broadway or Not To Broadway

An additional nugget of information. Yes, the dream to be on Broadway is a valid and wonderful one; however, there is a weighing of what you may give up in order to live that dream. It is a rare actor who gets to Broadway without an agent, so an actor must have one. I know one actor who moved a basket across the stage in one scene and sang in two chorus numbers in *Les Misérables* for twelve years. That was what he did for every show. It never changed. He had a paycheck and benefits and was on Broadway, but he gave up many other opportunities to audition for other work as he relied on being in that show. He has no experience in film to speak of now and as he had not auditioned for much in those twelve years he was very out of the loop when *Les Misérables* closed and he came back to the daily reality of getting acting work. I do not think he regrets his twelve years on Broadway, but I know he has had many difficult years since then booking any other paying work. Weigh the time required for the projects you do. Weigh what other things you may miss out on, or chose not to do, and how it will impact your career.

The other side of that coin is that I have another dear friend who has toured with *The Lion King* for over fifteen years all over the world and has also made time to do it on Broadway, work in films and have a great family. I am pretty sure he holds the record for the most performances in the role of Pumba, the warthog. He has made sacrifices as well and he has the most amazing wife ever, which helps, but this is a very happy man with his own choices, a man who could leave the show tomorrow and be right back out getting work immediately. He kept in the loop as he did this show; he did other small projects when he could (he did not rest on his laurels) and only missed out on the things he chose to. Weigh the odds in your own career and plan well. You can find the balance between Broadway and a career, but priorities must be figured out and having a real life offstage is a plus.

4

BEFORE ANY AUDITION

I auditioned for everything in the beginning. If they would let me
in the door, I would do it. Male roles, female roles, dogs, cats!
John Ritter, Cal-arts lecturer 1982–1983

If I were a young actor who had bought this book I would approach
this chapter and use it before a live film or stage audition and a self
taped one. Every audition you will ever do is an entire performance,
whether it is live or taped. Both require the same amount of preparation of text and yourself as well as some real technical knowledge.
However, first we must talk about something else that happens to
actors both in live auditions and with self taped ones. Fear. With the
increased technology actors now deal with due to self-taping and so
forth I see more fearful actors on film and live in auditions than ever
before.

Stage fright is something every actor has had and that a few actors
actively battle on a daily basis, and there is truly a way to think about
it differently. Many actors battle it, think about it, talk about it all the
time, and thus they give it growing power and can even seem to be
ruled by it. It can often cripple or ruin a career. Fear, my theory says,
is a very primal emotion that comes from way back when we all were
cave people and we lived in the lovely cave where it was warm and
snuggly and then one day someone went outside and 'stage fright'
kicked in – "What are you doing?! Something will eat you soon!!
Pay attention!!" That is what their brain screamed at them. That is
what stage fright (and fear in general) really is, a very primal protective
mental and emotional mechanism saying, "Focus. Pay attention.

Do not trip over the big lighting cable or whack the $20,000 camera with your hand. Do not walk off the edge of the stage and into the orchestra pit." Actors, you must learn to welcome your nerves and stage fright – seriously, they are working *for* you and the minute you inhale deeply and treat them as old friends you will not only be much calmer, but you will be much more focused. Fear is your friend, it helps you to focus. When stage fright shows up, take a deep breath and say, "Thank god for this, now I am focused." The acceptance of the fear will calm it right down and will also increase your own confidence and focus. Own your fear – do not let it own you.

Your Actor Toolbox in Digital Form

Part of being prepared for any audition is also taking yourself and your work very seriously. Another aspect to take seriously is even before the physical audition when you submit your materials, now mostly via email with digital files. The standard smallest size for digital files of your headshot is about 100 KB. Email it to yourself to check it out and click on it. You need to be able to see the entire headshot completely without any scrolling. You want to see your face and only your face immediately without having to scroll because the file is too big. If I get a headshot where I open the picture and only see part of an ear or some hair, I delete it and most casting directors will too. Also, please only send your resume as a PDF file. A reel is not best sent as an attachment to anyone at any time, as many email pro-grams will block it or strip it from the email, but sent as a link either to a YouTube or Vimeo video. All of this is part of your digital portfolio and needs to be organized and sendable from your iPad, smartphone, or computer with everything in the correct size and format needed.

Most working actors also keep an audition log or audition calendar. Why is this a smart idea? With an audition calendar you can keep track of when and where you audition and see how many jobs you book and also how often you do an audition for whom. An audition log is even better. Treated like a spreadsheet, it tracks dates, locations and who you see at what agency for what role for your auditions – add in the role for which you auditioned, any callbacks you had, if you got put on hold, who all the folks were in the audition room, if you booked the job, when the shoot dates were, the rate of pay, whatever you like.

It is great to be able to sit and review these logs and realize that the same casting director has called you in three times (which means they like you, but they are just trying to find the right thing to cast you in) or that you have had two calls for the same TV show in two weeks. You can map your own actor trends (out of how many auditions do you get a callback? Out of how many callbacks do you book a role?) and almost begin to predict who will cast you and when. Again, smart actors keep these types of logs (with people, roles, audition dates and locations) in order to map and see their own trends and opportunities, as well as to be well organized and prepared. Many of the apps mentioned in this book can act as your audition logs as well.

When I see an actor who has no digital or even physical portfolio or even a simple folder in their arms with their headshots, resume, copies of their audition monologues or the audition scenes, I wonder how committed and organized they really are on the stage or on sets. Be professional and organized always, as it carries over into your brain and confidence and how you carry yourself walking into the audition room. We take your work seriously only if you do.

Your Actor Toolbox in Physical Form

Please also carry your 'actor bag' with you at all times to auditions as well. It should contain:

1. At least two hard copy headshots with your resumes cut to 8 × 10, and stapled on the back. Do not ever have your resume be larger than your headshot. Ever
2. Copies of any audition monologues you use. (Have them on top of your bag if you get a last minute panic about what the first line of your monologue is – just look down at your bag and you can see it.)
3. A copy of whatever scene or monologue you have been sent for whatever audition you are going to. Make your own copy. Work on it, mark it up.
4. Water, juice, hydration.
5. A few granola bars or snacks.

6. Advil or Tylenol, and feminine hygiene products for girls.

7. A second top, in case you rip or spill on the one you have.

8. Hair brush, hair ties, shaver for men. Be prepared to touch up.

9. Your phone or iPad or both. Have your headshot, resume, reels and links to any websites (your own actor site or your YouTube channel) on both of these in textable and emailable digital form.

10. Reading material for any waiting you may have to do. See the suggested playlist at the end of this book. Read plays and screen-plays. If music focuses you or gets you in a pumped mood then have your iPhone loaded up with it.

11. Cough drops and/or any personal favorites needed.

12. Maps. In New York have both a subway and a bus map; in Los Angeles get a *Thomas Guide*. Know exactly how to get to and from your auditions.

13. Extra funds for the subway or the taxi if subways are down. Extra funds for gas or oil in Los Angeles.

14. Identification. Now that sounds odd, but in a few buildings in both Los Angeles and New York, especially post 9/11, you will be asked to show ID to enter. In Los Angeles and New York you may also have studio lot auditions, and you had better have your ID to get on the lot or in the building. In Los Angeles you may have driven and so you may have your driver's license on you. No matter where you are you should always carry your ID. It does me no good as a casting director for you to show up two hours late because you had to go home and get ID and come back and then enter the building.

This is part of how to prepare in a way that gets you the job. Casting directors *love* prepared actors. Prepared actors are serious actors. If you are prepared in the audition then I know you will be prepared on the set or in the rehearsal room. If you are prepared you can focus and be confident in an audition. I cast actors who are prepared.

Know that the casting people you meet truly want nothing more than for you to be really good, for you to be 'the one', if only so they can cast you and then have lunch and relax! You have no idea how much we are on your side. So you be on our side. Do your research about the writer or playwright. Research the casting person, what did she/he last cast? If any of the people at the audition have a gender neutral name (Terry, Sandy or the like), be sure you do not say you are here to see Mr. Smith if Mr. Sandy Smith is a female. If you are reading for an existing show on TV, then please watch it and understand what it is about. There is nothing worse than auditioning an actor who knows nothing about what they are reading for, nor whom they are reading for, or viewing a film clip where an actor has not fully prepared for an audition. An actor who wastes time like this does not get cast.

Also know about the technology involved in the show or project. Is there computer generated imagery? Is there blue screen or green screen technology used? Talking about that in the audition lets us know you did your research about it. Be awake and aware. Dead eyes, face or voice do not get you the job. Mispronouncing words in the text, or even the director's name, does not get you the job. Telling the director that you loved her last film and then naming a film she did not direct does not get you the job. Reading like every other actor who has auditioned that day does not get you the job. Giving a 'perfect' audition does not often get you the job.

Audition Material Preparation Exercises

So, when you prepare the audition scene or monologue, work on this:

1. Be specific: how do you feel about the other character in the scene with you? How do you feel about anyone else mentioned in the scene? How do you feel about the locations in the scene that you speak of? What about the objects mentioned? Know the specifics and how you feel about them. Why? Well, if I asked you, you as a person, if you liked or hated ten things and I just rattled off ten items you would be able to say, "Love him, hate that food, loved that movie, do not like her . . .", and so forth. You would not even have to think about it, you would have an immediate gut reaction and it would show in your responses. You should then have an equal gut reaction to every person, place or thing in the audition scene as well so that your scene is as specific as you are in real life. It is not enough to show up and be charming.

2. Look for the beats and the pauses and how to act them. Which are pauses and which are really beats? Sometimes they are written there in the text, but you can and should also add them. Look for acting moments that may not be obvious in the text. The actors who teach us something new about the scene, who create moments we have not thought of yet, they are the ones who get cast. Also, what is the difference between a beat and a pause? You see both of them in scripts and screenplays and many actors and directors treat them exactly the same. However, I have a theory that they are not the same. A pause is usually a fast moment, and we pause for many reasons. Perhaps we forget a word, get distracted, have another thought, etc., so we pause briefly. It is hard to act a short pause (you can act a long one, though). A beat (as well as the first moment in a scene or play being called an acting 'beat') when written in a script is very actable as it usually is a moment of transition. A transition from one thought to another, one emotion to another, etc. And it is supremely actable. Beats not written in the text can be inserted by the actor, and indeed those who do this often get the role. Usually the word 'but' comes after an actable beat. "I hate you, but I love you." (I act the beat before this 'but' often for my students to illustrate this.) Be on the lookout for this in the text.

3. Read your lines and think about the obvious emotional choices, the choices every single other actor will think of and make, then do the opposite. Or at least do something very different. Surprise us.

4. Read the other characters' lines, not just your own, and analyse their behavior – what is it you do or say that makes them respond how they do? What clues can their lines or behavior give to your behavior in the scene? If you read their lines and think, "Jeez, he is so defensive." Then that is a clue. What are you doing to make him so defensive? If you can tell in the scene, are you the protagonist? Are you the antagonist? Think about it. These clues are actable moments and elements you can show us.

5. In emotional scenes *do not* focus on or worry about that emotion or that is all you will do. Your brain will literally countdown to that crying (or shrieking, or falling to the floor, etc.) moment. Do not save your energy and focus for the emotion, but put it into

the choices and being specific about how you feel and what you want. As a young actor in my twenties I blew more than a few auditions because I could cry on cue. All my energy would be focused on that moment of crying and I would let all the other moments and choices fade away. Once I figured out that I was doing that, I stopped immediately. If I got to the emotional moment and cried, great, and if I did not that was great too, because I was still somewhere interesting due to the fact that I was specific and clear about my acting choices for the scene.

6. Stakes must be high in this scene. What do you want and what happens if you do not get it? If the stakes do not seem high, then embellish in your head so that they are and it matters to you. You are only interesting if the scene *matters* to you. I once had a student who had a film audition and in the scene she had to ask a man for money. That was it, two pages of her trying to get someone to give her money. So as we wanted her to stand out we gave her stakes. I said, "If he does not give you this money you might have to prostitute yourself." That raises the stakes. However, she then asked why would she prostitute herself? I then replied that maybe she had four kids under the age of ten and if she did not get the money she really would prostitute herself so she had money for a hotel room. For more urgency I asked her to imagine her kids were waiting across the street, alone, at a dingy donut shop with who knows bothering them. With these conditions the scene blossomed and became important and very urgent. Her stakes were high and her acting choices mattered. As long as the stakes are high in your mind, we (the casting people) do not need to know what they are, and they do not have to be in the text. Casting directors will not care what you made up or why, only that you were brilliant in the scene.

7. Button the scene. This is vital to any film audition in particular. If you have the last line in the scene then stay present in the scene and act until they say cut. If someone else has the last line then react to it and put a button, or closure on your work, do not just simply fade out. Your audition is not over until you leave that room and if they keep the cameras rolling for fifteen seconds after your last line (or your readers last line) you had better be present and acting, just like you would be on the film set.

8. Be different in choices, ideas, feelings, backstory and acting choices. Do not do the obvious or the easy. Be different if for no other reason than you will stand out from everyone else. Sometimes simply the act of standing out gets you the job.

9. Take risks, like taking your time, *do not* rush – find the acting moments and act them. Do not rush. Risk being opposite to everyone else. An actor who knows how to use time to think, especially for a film audition, is a joy.

10. You must be different to get cast. They must feel that you are fiery, smart, interesting and different, and then they will cast you. Find ways to be different in that scene. A great way to be different is to act beats in the text as mentioned before. If I see a line that is great in a scene and then I watch thirty actors not think and just read it, that is boring. How wonderful is it then when an actor comes in who is different, who inserts their own beat before the 'but' in that sentence and acts that transition?

11. Look for repetition in scenes and text. Repeated lines, phrases, words. Usually they are not written in the text by accident so if your character keeps saying, "By gum!" you need to work with it and make it yours – it is not a throw away line.

12. Have a question. Show them you have thought about the scene. When they ask, "Do you have any question about the scene/script/character?", have one. Many times if you have the one perceptive question of the day that alone will get you a callback. Once I walked into a film audition, aware that I was the last actress being seen for the role, and when he asked me, "Do you have any questions?", I said yes, and proceeded to ask a question about the character: wasn't she a local gal who grew up there and got elected sheriff and so wouldn't she have a Kentucky accent? His jaw dropped and he said in amazement that he had seen forty actresses that day and not one had asked him that, but that yes, she was indeed local and she would have an accent. I then read the scene with a Kentucky accent and walked out of the audition knowing that I had booked that role.

13. Look for the arc in audition monologues or scenes. Simple but effective. How are you different at the end of the monologue or scene from how you were at the start? What is the arc of that change? Is it slow? Is it abrupt? Does it happen mid-sentence?

Mid-word? Is it a slow boil that creates a change? Sometimes in a pinch of a cold read just playing the arc of a nicely written chunk of text can get you the job. How do you change in that text and when?

14. Stage work and film work is very different. Do not approach both with the same methodology. Your face and voice are much more subtle and contained in film work. Film work is filtered through a camera and director. Film work is 'real' and should feel as if it is you not acting at all. If you think it, the camera knows it. Stage acting should also feel 'real' but with a heightened sense of sharing the realness with 5,000 people who are listening in. Stage work is also filtered through a director, but at the end it is live and between you and the energy of the audience.

15. Listen to other actors and eavesdrop. Yep. I always lean against the wall of the room the actual audition is happening in. If you know that you and the other fifteen people are all auditioning for the same role with the same scene, you can listen for 'habits' in other people's auditions that can then help you in yours. For example, if there is a line in the scene written as, "I HATE YOU AND YOU SHOULD DIE!!!", then there are obvious choices an actor might make in relation to that. If you listen and you hear every single actor before you scream that line, then you need to walk in there and whisper it. If I am a casting person who has sat through twenty people screaming a line and you come in and do not scream it, I will love you just simply for being different. Do not let your audition be driven by what is on the page and seems obvious. Go fast, go slow. Be different.

16. Know the technology involved in the project. Are you acting with CGI characters? Is one of your arms a cyborg arm that is blue screened? Are you dealing with life size puppets or motion capture? Know about the project and technology and ask questions about it. We loved informed actors.

What about dress in auditions? Do not wear uniforms or costumes (especially for stage auditions), but you can dress to approximate how the person might look on their day off. If you are auditioning for a cop, do not wear a police uniform, but what that cop might wear on his day off. Other casting folks may disagree, but an actor who goes overboard and wears a full costume for the role does not impress me. Well, not unless they are a brilliant actor, but what they wear has nothing to do with that.

Of course there are time differences in preparation of an audition depending upon how far in advance you get the text or scene. If you get it one week in advance you can work your way through the exercises and notes above, as well as look up any words and research the project. If you get the audition scene one day in advance, what are the three things of the above list that you can use to prepare? Specifics, stakes, and acting the beats and pauses. If you walk in with that you will do well.

Printing out your copy of the audition scene is essential. When you print out your audition text you can then make notes, highlight your lines, map out choices and moments, circle new words you need to pronounce right. Yes, they usually will have extra copies of that scene at the audition, but you cannot mark on them, fold them or anything else. Also, as a casting person if I see actor after actor walk in with the same pristine piece of paper that I know we printed out as an extra copy, that tells me they did not bring their own copy and probably did not think much about, or work on, the scene. However, if I see an actor come in with their own copy printed out, marked up and written on I am immediately interested in what they may bring to the table. Another good reason to print out your own copy, and this is a big psychological one, is that when you finally thank everyone (and really, everyone) and you leave the building, head to the first garbage can you find and tear that audition scene up and toss it in. Let it go. Mentally and emotionally, as much as you can, let it go (and yes, it is hard, I know). If you get a callback and they want that same scene you can print it out again. Move on to the next audition, the next gig, but let it go.

Audition Monologues You Do

Is the monologue you do even the right audition material for you? If you continually do not get cast, then it is not. If you do not have a memorized monologue in your back pocket, you do need one. Try to find monologues you can flip to do both serious and comedic work all in one piece. Look at literature and books you read for underused text. Find a monologue in a book that works for you. Does it have to be the same sex, age and race as you? Heck no. If it works for you then use it – it will not matter if an eighty year old black woman said it in the book and you are a Vietnamese twenty year old guy with one leg. If it works for you, use it. If it works for you, then it works for us watching you do it.

Look at plays over ten years old if you look in theatrical works – do not do the current Tony winner texts. Find different and older plays and scripts. Breaking out of the monologue stereotype box, especially for women (as less is written for female actresses), means you can take a look into male monologues. One of my long term students, a lovely young black woman, does an amazing Hamlet's soliloquy and is about as different from Hamlet as you can get. Her walking and talking through that Hamlet monologue, though, causes it to become about her and her life and her choices as a black woman. We forget that it is a Danish prince. Very powerful stuff and a real attention grabber in an audition.

Keeping 'live' for film and stage auditions is also a job getter. Be real, be true, with all your quirks and sneezes and reality. Do not give a perfect audition, especially for film. 1940s films are not the way to go compared to now, as actors then were perfect, not a hair out of place, and never stretched, sneezed, or farted. In 2018 the fun is being real or even ugly. Sneeze, itch, lean back, be real. Interrupt, shake things up, ask questions. Make contact. Look us in the eyes. Be a real human being. One way to shake us up is not to do one of my pet peeves. An actor who is auditioning and sees a scene where he has to interrupt another actor usually tries to be polite in the audition. So, if the other actor has a line like this:

Actor 1: I hate her. I absolutely do not like –

Then what I see 90 percent of the time is Actor 2 waiting until the first actor has said 'like' and then pausing and then saying his next line. Wrong. We do not interrupt like that in real life. When I act or direct I have actors look for two words before the dash and start their line there. So, if I was reading this scene I would interrupt the above line:

Actor 1: I hate her. I absolutely do not like –

And I would interrupt it on the word 'do' so that I really am interrupting. Stop being polite when you act, stop taking turns. Be real. That is what you reflect as an actor.

When I see an actor who seems to be very talented (they are a good reader, good actor, good person) and they do not book the work and they are trying to figure out why, it is either because they have some behavioral issue that is a no-no in auditions, like forcing handshakes on everyone to be polite, or because they are a chronic 'perfect' auditioner. They take turns when they read, they make the safe and polite choices as an actor. They even 'act' politely in their characters and choices. Boring. Do not ever be perfect, the goal is to be real and alive, not perfect. Perfect is boring. Perfect is not what we cast.

When is the time the audition really starts? It starts way before you actually enter the audition room. Start your audition in your head the minute you leave your house. No matter what city you live and work in, no matter where you audition, it is a very small world. Everyone in this industry in your city knows each other. With every single audition you build a reputation. Even if you believe that the script that you are auditioning with is the worst text ever, do not judge it. Treat it as if it is the best. Treat the person that you are reading the scene with (and sometimes the audition reader is great and sometimes they are awful) as if they are Meryl Streep. I know a director in Los Angeles who uses horrible scenes and monologue scripts to audition actors because he wants to see if they make the text better, and also to see if they walk in 'in judgement' of the text. A good actor makes any text better and shows us new things in it. Be that actor.

Your Digital Footprint

Next to your digital footprint on social media, equal in importance is creating an actor website. Weebly and many other sites will give you a free website with up to five pages and constructing it is pretty user friendly. What should an actor have on their website? Let's say you have five free pages you can use. The main page has your best headshot or two, name, a brief bio and either your resume embedded in the page for easy viewing or a link to it. Page two can be your media page with links to your reels (which should be on your YouTube channel) and extended clips of the scenes from which the clips in your reel came. Any moving media (other film, TV, etc.) could go on page two. Page three can be a 'gallery' page where the rest of your headshots and any other photos taken in different roles, on stage or on set, can be put. Page four can be used for your other talents (stunt reel and resume or voice over reels and resume, audiobooks, modeling or singing work) and page five could be used for news and links to your films as they go to festivals or to plays you are in and where to get tickets. On that last page, or on all the pages, have a "Contact Me" link so you can always be reached. Of course an actor can have fifteen pages or more on their website, but the bigger it is the less time we will spend on it, so keep it smaller and very updated, and make sure the best stuff is in the first few pages.

Have all reels, pics and resume on your phone at all times, I cannot say this enough. A new trend is going to always be an app. Not all apps are great, though. The Clapit app associated with *Backstage* is a new media development and is setting a new and dangerous precedent for auditioning and acting. Clapit began as an app where you would applaud things and people you loved online. In 2017 it began to become a new way of casting:

> **NEW YORK – Aug. 24, 2017** – *PRLog* – In conjunction with the production release of his next film, Producer Russ Emanuel announced today a nationwide open call for actors to submit auditions for one male and one female speaking role via the social media app Clapit. The film, *"Lighter Than Air,"* will be shot in Los Angeles in October. All auditions must be submitted through Clapit in accordance with Clapit's competition rules, terms and guidelines. To support the open call for his next film, *"Lighter Than Air,"* Russ Emanuel has partnered with the social media entertainment network Clapit, where emerging performance artists can be discovered via an innovative, community-driven audition process from their mobile devices.

Hmmmm. Should you get the app? It is not imperative now, but it may be in another year when more and more casting is decided upon it. Unfortunately it then becomes about who is the most popular person and has the most active social media followers; it does not mean who is the most talented, and nor does it mean all those 'followers' will watch whatever film the person is cast in. *Backstage*, arguably the most well known casting platform around, has now in 2017 begun posting Clapit casting notices, which is sending a dangerous message about popularity and social media casting. I hope the trend will not grow, but I fear it will. Social media has a power that you must be a part of.

Social Media and Branding

In this century most actors should also be aware of 'branding' and what 'brand' they present. A brand is a way of marketing yourself so that what you offer is immediately recognizable and sellable to others. It is a way of differentiating between you and other actors. A voice over student of mine brands himself as the 'voice of science-fiction and fantasy.' And it works for him. A marketing and branding plan for an actor may also include your presence on Facebook, Instagram, Twitter, Pinterest, YouTube, Vimeo, Google+, LinkedIn, Tumblr, Reddit, Snapchat and many more. What makes you different? What is your brand? Are you the accent master? Why should I hire you and not someone else? Knowing what is special about yourself is always a good thing.

Preparing Accents for Film or Stage

On the subject of accents and how to deal with them in any medium, there are differences between film and stage accents. I am not a fan, as a casting director, of actors who do bad or no accents. I have a pet peeve of seeing actors audition for a role that has an accent if they do not do the accent. I, in fact, detest when an actor asks if they should do the accent, when I have posted in the audition notice specifically that the role has an accent. If the role has an accent do the accent, *always*. You can get away with what I call a 'gloss' for film auditions, which is a subtle and rough version of the accent, yet is enough for me to know that you could do it well if I cast you and had you coached. For a stage production audition I want to hear a fairly near perfect accent or I most likely will not cast you. A film may have an accent coach budget, but a play may not (and the accent must be sharper and better to carry in a large theater as opposed to on camera), so that is why the different standard between stage and film is applied. There are horror stories of films where actors have terrible accents, but much fewer stories of stage actors having them. This is why. Again, help the casting people to cast you by doing what you do well.

5

THE AUDITION:
FILM AND TV

You just keep it up. Keep auditioning. If you have the talent then you will book the gig.

Tony Randall, actor

Marks, frames and slates, oh my!

One thing before we jump right into film and TV auditions. Many times I encounter young actors who seem to feel that the casting people are their enemies. I have heard many an actor over the years complain that they were not liked as they were made to read the scene three whole times. Let me impress this upon you a second time; after you read a scene or monologue in an audition there are two things the casting person can say. They can say, "Thank you", and show you the door. Or they can say literally anything else and anything other than showing you the door is a huge win. Asking you to read more than once is a huge win. They want you to be great, so do not treat them as opponents.

Them giving you a note in an audition and asking you to read again is enormous. It means they do like you and that they want to establish two things. One, can you listen to that note that they gave you, and two, can you take direction. Listening is an enormous task for a young actor, especially if you are in the middle of a nerve-wracking audition. Let's assume you have read well and I want to see if you can listen and follow directions, so I ask you to read it a second time and to be angrier. You appear to be listening, you nod your head enthusiastically and you then read the scene *exactly* the same way you read it the first time. So I likely may not cast you, because I know that you do not listen. There is a useful trick to being able to listen while your brain is freaking out and telling you, "My God!!! I am auditioning for Spielberg!" As Mr. Spielberg asks you to read it again, but angrier, you immediately repeat back to him what he has asked you to do. "Alright, I will read it again, but be angrier. Got it." He hears this and loves that you have listened to him, and by your repeating it aloud you have made your own brain stop screaming nervously and listen, so that it knows what it is doing next. Then you read the scene, you are angrier in it, and you both listened to him and took the direction he gave you and so you get cast. Film auditions are very different from stage. In a film audition we need to know you can do the role tomorrow with very little or no rehearsal. That is why we need to see you can listen and adjust, and we need to see it in the audition.

> Sometimes when actors don't get the part, it's not always about an actor being a bad actor; it's about connecting to the material.
>
> Linnea Berthelsen

Controlling Your Audition

Camera choreography is also something that a model understands that many actors do not. If you are in a close up shot and the camera lens is focused to inches in front of your face, you must be able to understand 'camera choreography' and how to move. Even if you hold your neck and head completely steady as you speak, you can still blow the camera choreography in a shot with quick eye shifts or rapid facial movements.

Something that I love when an actor auditions is when they take control of their own audition and the room and whatever else they need. Most actors are unfailingly polite. I can set a chair directly in the actor's way in the middle of the room, have fifty actors audition that day and not one will move the chair or even ask if it is alright to move it, even if it is in their way. Move the darn chair, folks. Move your reader as well if you need to (if you have a great left side of your face but your reader is standing on your left so you have to have your right side to the camera, just ask the reader sweetly to move. They will and we will love that you took control). Move the chairs, be in control of your audition. By controlling your audition you are able to have things how you need them to be so that you can show us your best self, and that is what I want to see. Unfailingly polite actors are boring. Show me who you are, be brave, change my mind about the role. Move the chair.

There are many real life stories where film casting completely changed because of an actor. Actors can walk into an audition and change minds about race, gender and sometimes even age for a role. Actors can walk into an audition and change the dialogue as well. In film auditions some of the time there is only a rough working script that has not been finalized yet. Often you are reading rough drafts in your audition and any ad libs you put in may make it into the final script. There have even been times (very shady times) that auditions have been had in order to see how the text feels and what ad libs might come out of it, without actually casting any of the actors seen. I have also many times seen a rough script becoming much less rough and changing to a very defined text as the actors cast brought themselves to the project. Actors in films can literally change the entire film script by showing up and showing themselves.

One of the most difficult things to do as an actor is to just walk into an audition room and be yourself in control. How do you do that? What do you do with your hands? Should you walk in the manner of the character you are auditioning for? Should you walk calmly or with energy? How can you walk like you and relax? First, realize it is *you* we want to see walking in, not the character you are auditioning for. We need to see you first as a person before we can see you in the role. Take a deep breath, relax and just walk in the door and you will be fine. Imagine you are going to hang out with some people you like. We need to see you, the real you, especially for TV work as TV has a notoriously short rehearsal time, or no rehearsal at all, and thus most actors are cast on their personality and charisma coming in the door. Oh, and yes, some talent too.

Marks and How To Work Around Them: An Exercise

Marks are the marks taped on the floor (in the shape of an X or T) used in filmed media and are important to 'hit', whether in an audition (when you stand on it so you are in focus) or in filming. You can practise an exercise at home, hitting marks like the professionals do without looking at them. On the set, and in your practice, you should use eye level references while you are actually on your physical mark so that you can minimize looking down at the mark in the scene. I may have my mark on the floor but I will pinpoint another visual or physical reference, maybe I am six inches from the edge of the book-case, so I never have to look down at the mark on the floor as I move to it or to my next mark. Practise this at home by taping four or five marks on the floor (either in an X or a T shape, again) around a room and pacing through a scene or monologue with them. Getting good at this will enable you to do it in auditions and callbacks as well as on the actual set.

As mentioned, reaction shots are the lifeblood of TV in the 21st century. Practise a few exercises at home that teach you how to relax normally and to react. A great exercise is to film yourself watching the last ten minutes of a movie that you have never seen before. Film ten minutes of you watching the end of a good comedy, ten minutes of the end of a good drama and ten of the end of a good horror film. Then watch the film of yourself – how is it that you react to these emotions and situations? How is it you react in real life? How do others react? What do people do when they listen? What do they do with their hands, their mouths, their heads, their eyes? What do people do when they pretend to listen, but really are not? You must be an avid observer of people in order to be an actor. How else can you reproduce moments on film or stage?

> Good acting – real acting is impossible to spot. Do you ever catch talents like Robert Duvall or Kathy Bates acting? No. I defy you to show me where.
>
> William Esper

Slating and Making It Count

Slating is not only something you do and say to the camera before you read your audition text, it is another part of your complete audition. One New York casting director does not have his camera person film the audition scene, only the slates. He then casts only from the energy he sees in the slates, and he casts some wonderful actors. Many actors treat slates, "Hi, my name is John Smith and I will be reading the part of Ben," as something unimportant and unenergized. They save their focus for the scene they audition with. Big mistake. (As a side note if you are agented state your agency or agent after your name in the slate. Do not make them search for your agent's name.) Any time you look into the camera you must be connected to it and slating is your first chance to do that in any audition. Use that slate with energy and connect into that camera as if there was someone inside it, because later when we all sit around and watch the auditions we will see that connection or the lack of it. Another terrific way to use slates is to do them the opposite of your audition scene energy. For example, if I know the audition scene I am reading is very dramatic and dark then I will do my slate in a more fun, upbeat energy and then go right into the dark audition scene. And vice-versa, if my audition scene is heavily comedic I will be very serious with my slate. Note, I said serious, not unenergized or boring. Make us pay attention from the slate on. Grab us from "Hello".

Connecting and Crying

One of the things I get asked about a lot in both auditions and performing is crying and I do not mean dry crying. Crying is a natural emotion that comes from an actor being connected to the text and to their own acting abilities. Dry crying is something where you contort your face and make fake crying noises, but nothing is really happening inside. While dry crying can get you (rarely) an Oscar nomination (see, for example, dry crying in *Gorillas in the Mist* when the main gorilla dies and the leading lady dry cries on film and it is embarrassing to see), it is never as good as being fully present emotionally in your performance or audition. In order to cry real tears, you must be connected to the material and you must honestly open yourself and your own emotions to it. Emotional recall exercises can help with this. Find true things that trigger tears or laughter and use them in your work. Ground it in your reality. Over time you will no longer need the emotional triggers as you learn how your emotional instrument works and how to use it from your own experienced emotions.

Filmed audition scenes also ask you to make connections. Reading to the camera in an audition does not lessen the impact, nor does it require less energy because it is not a real person; you just simply treat the camera as if it is a person and connect more with it. If you have a 'reader' in the audition, you treat them well (you could always offer to shake their hand, as most actors treat them like furniture) as they could either be just a person filling in or they could be the actual actor cast in that role. In any audition realize that everyone in the room has heard the scene at least forty times even before that audition day. They heard it in draft form, in earlier meetings, and from other actors. They know the most obvious ways to perform it, and they have seen that already many, many times before you enter the room. I have even seen casting directors unconsciously mouth the lines along with the actors, not even realizing it because they have seen that scene so many times. They really are looking for something different, real, surprising, funny, unperfect. Connect with the text, the reader and your own emotions, and you will be what they are looking for.

The Secret Power Behind You Getting Cast

There is also a secret power behind who gets the part, and this is applicable to all media auditions as well as stage auditions. Most actors have no idea that a person they either ignore or treat very badly may be the person who controls their fate. This is the unsung hero, the audition monitor. When you arrive at your audition, most of the time there is a person there to check you in, ask you if you need a copy of the audition text, tell you where the restroom is and manage all the actors. I recommend you always listen to and remember that person's name. They are vital. Treat them with the highest regard. You should treat everyone well anyway. After your audition is done, go and find that person and say thank you to them in a very sincere way. Why? Because they work hard and it is a good policy to always say thank you. Also, when all the actors have gone home and we sit around to cast the actors, we always call in that audition monitor. She or he is the only one of us who has seen all the actors outside the audition room, behaving as they really are.

I cannot tell you how many times, when deciding between two actors, the audition monitor will pipe up and say, "Oh my god, that guy. He was fifteen minutes late and hit on all the girls in the hall." Guess who does not get cast? That guy. If you behave badly in the hall, that is most likely how you will behave on the set if cast. The audition monitor is asked about actors all the time. I have also seen it work the other way when deciding between two actors; the audition monitor will say, "Oh, she was great. Out of the whole day she was the only one who said thank you to me." So then we cast that girl. If the audition monitor recommends someone, we cast them. If they do not, we really do not cast them. Often the audition monitor may also be the stage manager or one of the producers or even a fellow filmmaker, so always treat them with the respect they deserve.

What about stage directions in auditions? By this I mean the very dramatic stage directions, in parenthesis like so: "(She grabs the knife and the gun and stabs him and then shoots him fourteen times, screaming at the top of her lungs with each bullet!)"; or another wonderful one like this: "(He falls to the floor suddenly, sobbing hysterically and heavily)". These types of stage directions in auditions really should be totally ignored by actors – and, yes, I know there is one casting person out there yelling, "No! That's wrong!" But that is the only one. I have seen actors try to pull off these types of stage directions and it rarely – and I mean rarely – works. Why?

Imagine it from our side, the casting side. We see a marvelous actor that we are enjoying like mad: they are real and relaxed and specific and great, and then, all of a sudden, they pull out the famous 'finger gun' and mime shooting the other actor. Or they go from being fascinating to lying on the ground fakely and dry crying. It ruins the scene in the moment and ruins it yet again as we replay it and watch it later on film. It can even make us not cast the best actor we see. Just do not do it. Let it go, trust me. We want to see the real you, not pantomime and over the top emotion. Just be where you are in that moment and let that stage direction go. You can worry about that high emotional moment at callbacks.

The types of film and TV that you may audition for can be from many genres (horror, science fiction, drama, etc.) and from many types of films (indies, student films, feature films, series, etc.) and even soap operas. What then are the differences in the acting styles for all of these? My thoughts are that, aside from small stylistic issues, they are all about acting truthfully; nevertheless, what they may look for in actors can vary widely. For instance, in a science fiction film or TV show, they want sharp and highly articulate actors. Technical and 'alien' dialogue requires actors (and often character actors) who are on point, speak well and who present as physically confident. For soap opera auditions, they will always be on the lookout for pretty actors who are great with acting 'reaction shots' (reaction shots again being when someone else is speaking but the camera is filming your reaction to it) and are very relaxed in manner. TV over the past ten years has become a medium of mostly reaction shots. Watch your favorite TV show and make a mark on paper every time there is a reaction shot. Now watch the very same episode and make a mark every time the camera remains on the person speaking until they are done speaking. I guarantee you there will be four to five times as many reaction shots. We are rapidly developing into an audience who listens very little and instead watches reactions more than actually thinking about the dialogue, and TV is the primary medium that caters to this.

A Bit about Yourself

An inevitable question for actors that comes up from casting directors in auditions for any type of media or stage is, "Tell me a bit about yourself." When a casting person asks this, actors can sometimes respond in one of two ways. They either say, "Uh . . . um . . . uh . . .", for way too long or they begin to recount the last play they did and who they played and what they did before that and who they played. Neither of these is the right answer. We do not ask this to hear you talk about your resume, nor do we ask it to put you on the spot as if this is a test. We have your resume in front of us so we are not concerned with that. What this question really means is, "Please tell us something about you, as a human being, that is unique and funny or sad and real and YOU." So how then should you reply in a way that is true, but that can also increase the likelihood of your getting the part?

> There's nothing more boring than unintelligent actors, because all they have to talk about is themselves and acting. There have to be other things.
>
> Tim Robbins, actor

What you want to say is something true and something that makes a moment of connection happen with the casting person. For example,

I have a student, a very big and buff fellow often cast as a bully or weightlifter, and he has a secret hobby. He loves to bake, and not only bake, but he loves to bake muffins. The minute he told me this I knew we had found his 'tell me about you' story. So that is what he tells them, about how his grandma taught him to bake and how he collects muffin recipes, and somewhere in the conversation there is a golden moment where the casting person forgets that he is an actor and forgets that they are even casting him and they simply say, "Oh, man, I love red velvet cupcakes!", and they both laugh and they connect. Two people *connect*.

If you can create a moment to connect with a director or casting person then you remind them that you are real and not just 'an actor'. You get them to like you as the real you and you also keep yourself in the room longer as you talk (which increases the likelihood of your being cast) and then they find that they really do like you and relate to you and all this is before you have even read the darn audition scene. So, help them to like 'you' as you, not the actor. Have one or two good stories to tell when they ask about you. Tell them about a trip that you took, languages that you speak, your pets ("I have fourteen gerbils!"), your hobbies, something cool that you did, but make it about you, the human being, not the actor. This is a way to be cast before you even read the audition scene. If they like you, they will most likely cast you. This also has a secondary outcome in that, if your story is interesting and you do connect with the casting person, you again remain in that casting room longer. The longer you stay in that room the greater your chances are of being cast and the more the actors waiting in the hall get psyched out. My buff student booked around 50 percent more work the minute he started telling this true story about himself and his love of baking when asked.

> Having auditioned many actors, I'm used to hearing ones that can take any writer's lines and make it sound like their own words. And I'm also used to less experienced (or less gifted) ones who sound uncomfortable with words that aren't their own. They sound as if they're are reciting or reading something. They sound scripted.
>
> Marcus Geduld, director

Film Versus Stage Language

Film has one other difference from stage and that is another language issue. Stage plays are of two kinds: well-known with well-known dialogue and roles, or totally new with new roles and dialogue. However, there is a reality with stage language that, even when it is bad (cursing, profanity, or gross or horrifying imagery in language), it still tends to be rooted in a 'stage awareness' of what will play to a live audience or can be supported visually or some other technical way on stage. Film is another story entirely in that it is well known for being able to show imagery that would be hard to deal with on stage. Imagine a film like *Hostel* or *Saw* or *Star Wars*, but performed live on stage. Even done well, it would be much tamer performed on a stage because its effect is rooted in film imagery and film language, meaning it is carried and shown best by that medium.

Thus, more so than in stage auditions, often in film auditions you will encounter language (whether profane or anti-religious or any variation of anti-something), imagery or ideas (maybe you audition and your cold read is a monologue about torturing someone that both is profane and has gross or disturbing imagery) that may be very hard for you, the person, to deal with. It may be hard to deal with for personal, religious or moral reasons. Decide before you ever encounter it how you will handle it. Decide it now, today, before it happens to you, so you can take it in stride without stopping the audition. Also, if you are in a motion capture or other technical audition, you really need to focus on the technical issues and have your script priorities set in your mind already as an actor. When confronted with disturbing, sexual, or profane, etc., texts, some options are:

1. Read it as written and be fine with whatever it is. It is not you, it is acting.
2. Read it and then mention after reading that, if you get cast, you would like it all changed.
3. Read it as written and, if you are cast, then ask them nicely to change a few lines or words.
4. Ask before reading it, as you glance at it, if you can change a few words in the audition.
5. Read it and, without asking, substitute words for the ones that disturb you in the text.

6. Tell them before reading it that, if it is disturbing or profane, you will have to stop reading immediately.

Now, all of these are very real options and by the time you do get handed any text, if you have read the film summary or a breakdown, you should already have a pretty good idea of whether or not there might be disturbing passages in it. If you have paid attention you will have a hunch. My own personal choice (as I get asked what I do when acting) as an actor is to just read it as written and commit fully to it. I do not make judgements about content when I audition, I just act. That is my choice as an actor, however, not yours.

As a casting person, though, I would say do either number 1 (read it as written), number 3 (as your request comes *after* you are cast when we really do like you and want to keep you), or number 5 (as often your in-the-moment word substitution may end up making the text better and could get you cast with some rewriting based on what you did in the audition). Number 2 has you asking them to change the text before you are even cast in the role and it is never wise, as then they will just not cast you most of the time. Let them cast you first. Number 6, while it may be the only choice for a few actors (for religious or moral issues), is not the best option; however, if you feel that strongly about it, then own it. Stop if you need to and thank the casting staff, but just say the language is not for you. They will respect you for it. They may not cast you, but they will respect you and your reputation. So, think about all that right now, before all the auditions happen. Be clear on the 'you' that you want to present to us and commit to it.

You may also be offered roles at times in your career that do not mesh with your moral or ethical standards, or you simply do not like the script. It may be badly written or gratuitous, with a lot of sex or violence. If that happens, do read the script, mull it over and, if you decide to turn it down, do so gracefully and gratefully. The project may become a hit without you or it may bomb, but be gracious in turning down any roles offered to you. I actually turned down an off-Broadway offer (with no audition at all) at one point in my career because the text just did not work for me on a few levels. But I adored the playwright and still do, and turned it down respectfully and with love. What did not work for me I knew would work for another actress and it did.

6

THE AUDITION: COMMERCIALS, INDUSTRIALS, NATIONAL CALLS

Most of the time what you'll be selling won't be your talent – it'll be your personality.

M. K. Lewis, teacher and author

Commercials

Commercials can be the lifeblood of many an actor's career. A national commercial can even pay for a year of your rent and lifestyle. Two or three national commercials can buy you a house. To get work in them on a consistent basis you not only must be talented, but a technical wiz at auditioning. You must also never forget that any commercial, no matter how fun or touching or digitally creative it is, is about selling the product. That means you are not the star. You are always a supporting player. I have an old college pal who teaches commercial acting in Los Angeles and is great at teaching and also booking the work herself. She knows how to sell things without seeming to. You trust her. You can become a viable commercial actor if you have the right looks and can read commercial copy to sell whatever product there is (although a little known actor fact is that, if you are under twenty-five years old, you cannot be hired to advertise alcoholic products in the United States. True!). However, the more you know the commercial market, the more you watch commercials with a critical eye and then practise, the better your chances are at being cast.

I went in for a cat food commercial and was completely memorized. They set up the take and the minute I opened my mouth

I blanked except for the first line. So, I said the first line and started improvising. I think I acted like the cat itself somewhere in there. They just sat, stunned, with jaws open. But, you know what? They loved it and called me two days later and I booked the job. Sometimes the biggest mistakes can be the thing that gets you the job.

Joni, student

Two of the five basic types of commercials are what I call 'Food', which means anything that is food and drink, and 'Products', which is anything else that is handheld and is a product (a bottle of Tylenol, an iPhone, makeup and the like). One of the things I see kill commercial auditions time and time again has absolutely nothing to do with the acting or even the reading of the text: it is the simple technical placement of the hand holding the product during the audition or callback. At times the hand holding the product may wobble or even drift out of the frame of the camera. This is an easy tip I teach my students for product auditions. If they hand you a product or a wooden block stand-in for it at the last moment, hold it in your dominant hand and your script in the other hand, and then quickly touch the product to your temple (a great way to remember this is that we think about buying products, so touch it to your brain). Next, move it six inches out to the side (left or right, put it in your dominant hand) and freeze that arm there until someone says cut. It then stays in frame at all times and you can focus on the text.

Exercise: Commercial Auditions for Food or Products

You can practise this arm motion at home: film yourself and train this to be an automatic movement that you do not even have to think about. It is also easier then if you want to look at the product, point to it or even talk to it in the commercial without moving it out of that frozen position. This keeps you in control of yourself, the text and the product. That control and confidence translates to your audition. In any audition you want to be in control of yourself, the text and the props.

The same basic rule applies for food or drink commercials. Touch it to your chin (and you can remember this as we taste foods, not think about them), then move it six inches out to either side and freeze that arm there. The minute your arm moves out of the frame with that product in it, chances are that you will not be hired. The product, or the food item, is always the star of the commercial, not you. You can practise this at home by watching in your bathroom mirror as well, even practising talking to the product or referencing it without moving it or your arm.

An extra note about food commercials. If you do book one and you have to eat the product in the commercial, you may then find that the writer has not quite thought that through. You may see something like this:

> Your line: The best burger ever!
> (Takes a huge bite of burger)
> You: Grab one today!

Hmmm, now the writer has not quite thought out how you are going to say the last line with a mouth full of burger, but you now have to do it. So – and yes, practise at home – take as small a bite as you can while making it look huge, and then stuff it into your cheek and then say the line. Another helpful tip if you book a food commercial: if you walk into the shoot and see bunches of burgers, or donuts, or whatever the commercial is about, then ask for a small trash can to be put around where you are filming. Believe me, on take twenty-two you will be glad you did not swallow all those bites of burgers, but instead spit them out into the trash can. I once did forty-seven takes for a local donut commercial (the director, cameraman and bakery owner could not agree on how the commercial could be) and, had an old stagehand not given me the wonderful advice to get a trashcan and spit the donut out between takes, I very well may have gotten sick by take ten.

Testimonials are a great kind of commercial in that usually you are the only one in it and you have all the lines, just you talking to the camera. They are usually intimate, often serious, and have a 'just between the two of us' feel. For any testimonial commercial auditions, you should memorize the text fully if at all possible. If it is only you on camera, you want to do it right, and you constantly pausing to look at your text will not work well. A great way to practise is to look in the mirror for focus as you do it. Put a dot on the mirror, make that your camera and play into it. Pick a person in your mind and imagine them in that camera so that you really connect. The trend in some current auditions is that many times you will be asked to improvise after the text ends. That exercise of looking at the pretend camera in the mirror will help with this as well. I have seen actors do a good testimonial audition and then lose it completely when asked to continue to improvise to the same camera while it films. Being camera conscious and also understanding camera choreography is essential.

Another great tip, especially for testimonials when you are looking into a camera a lot, is from the wonderful British actor Michael Caine. The tip (and the trick) is not to blink at all, or certainly to blink less. It takes some practice to learn controlled blinking, but it does help you as an actor to not break your camera eye contact with rapid or fast blinking. Now I do not think you necessarily need to do this tip every single moment you are ever on film, although that is what he says he has done in his very long career, but the tip is a great one for anything (testimonials or close ups, which are tightly framed) where you must look into the camera. Look for this when you film yourself, do you blink a lot? Do you blink rapidly when nervous? If so, start practising taking longer and more aware moments between blinks.

One of my favorite types of commercials is what I call the 'non-dialogue'. These are the types of commercials that involve you acting with things (elves, dragons and the like) that are not real, but are instead added later via CGI. The announcer dialogue also is added in later as an announcer type voice over. So, while you are sent a script, you do not have any lines and the script is usually a storyboard representation of how it will all look.

You will also know exactly what the announcer is saying over your actions; you just do not have any lines yourself. This is very freeing as there is nothing for you to memorize. So, in the actual audition, you go in and the auditioner reads the storyboard for you and you act it out while you are being filmed. Usually you will get up to four or five takes; they may tell you to look higher up where the CGI character might be added, or to be more or less expressive for one take, or things like this. It is great fun and you will usually spend ten

BOYLES FURNITURE
"LEG TO STAND ON"
TV: 30

OPEN ON MAN IN SUIT STANDING ON LEG, WITH OTHER LEG UP. HE'S HOLDING MONEY IN RIGHT HAND, AND LEG OF CHAIR IN LEFT HAND ABOVE HIS SHOULDER.

ANNOUNCER (VO):
When it comes to fine furniture, Boyles has <u>a leg up</u> on our competition.

DOLLY UP TO CHAIR MAN IS HOLDING. A WOMAN'S LEG CAN BE SEEN STANDING ON CHAIR.

We offer everyday savings of 40–50% OFF

DOLLY UP TO SALESWOMAN STANDING ON ONE LEG, AND HOLDING THE LEG OF A PIECE OF FURNITURE IN HER HAND ABOVE HER HEAD.

With selections from Drexel-Heritage, Thomasville, Baker and more ...

DOLLY UP TO REVEAL SOFA WHICH SALESWOMAN IS HOLDING ABOVE HER HEAD.

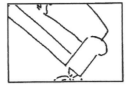

... you're certain to find a look that's you.

PAN LEFT TO REVEAL HAPPY DOG SITTING ON END OF SOFA.

When it comes to selection, sales and service ...

ZOOM OUT TO REVEAL ENTIRE STRUCTURE OF BALANCING ACT ON LEFT SIDE OF SCREEN, WHILE ALSO REVEALING ANNOUNCER IN CENTER, AND A SECOND BALANCING ACT ON RIGHT. RIGHT GROUP SUDDENLY COLAPSES AND COMES CRASHING TO FLOOR. SUPER: BOYLES LOGO AND for the look that's you.

... our competition really doesn't have <u>a leg to stand on.</u>

Boyles Furniture. <u>For the look that's you.</u>

Figure 6.1 Storyboard example

minutes or more in the room with the casting person or producer. This gives you more time, again, to connect with the auditioners as people. Often the producer you are in the room with is the very same person who will direct the commercial, so connecting is crucial. Just listen carefully to what they ask you to change, and act. Simple.

Practising Commercials at Home

When you do practise commercials, whether running dialogue or simply in front of a mirror to get camera focus, practise with products that you really do use in real life and that you like a lot. You want to be in the habit of feeling like you do commercials for things you love so that when you do audition you take the "I love this!" feeling into the audition and on camera with you. There is nothing worse than an actor auditioning for a product they do not use or understand, or even worse for a product they hate. Most of the time we can see it in the audition that they hate the product. It shows.

A great exercise to help you take the product love into your auditions is to write a commercial yourself, about a product you absolutely love and use yourself. Make it thirty seconds long or a minute long and then practise it. Then call a few friends over and perform it for them as if you really are doing it before a camera on a commercial shoot. Will they now buy it? Do they believe your opinion about it? Are they excited by your excitement about it? They need to be truthful about how your commercial makes them feel and, if they are not all sold on it and ready to run out and get it, you have some work to do.

I am often asked if there are certain hours not to audition for commercials, or for anything really? Oh yes, there are if you have any choice about it. Do not audition half an hour before lunch if you can because everyone in the room is hungry and has to pee. That is literally all they are thinking about. Half an hour after lunch they all are tired from eating and they are groggy. In both of these situations I have often seen terrific actors become not only ignored but forgotten completely after they have read, because the casting director was hungry, tired or had to pee or have a cigarette. Yep. Truth.

Industrial, Training, or Educational Films

I also tell my students to always audition for industrial films (sometimes billed as educational films, training films, in house films). There are many reasons to do these and they can be the gift that keeps on giving. Industrials may be infomercials or they may be in house films. Let us say Nike has a new shoe and they want a twenty minute in house shot film that explains how the shoe is made for their staff. This film will never leave the Nike corporation, never will be shown outside Nike facilities, but there are many reasons why you want to be in it. First, it pays well and you are treated well. You are usually paid a flat fee and flown to the headquarters of the company. It can take up to four or more days to film and you are in a lovely hotel all the while. Corporations are also well known for loading you down with the actual product, so then maybe you go home with eight pairs of Nikes. Also, to make certain you do not go film an in house film with Adidas the very next week, Nike will most usually give you a 'buyout' (they pay you to not do work with a competitor product) for six months or even a year or more. That is another chunk of funds on top of your filming fee. If that film works well in house you may get another yearly buyout and another and another.

As I said, industrials are the gift that can keep on giving. Perhaps your training film becomes an in house hit and when the company expands overseas you get another buyout on a larger scale and for a longer time period. I know an actor who has had more years than I can count, well over forty, on a buyout for an in house training film (and they do not even make the product the film is about anymore) that became part of the corporate culture to watch. The actor has just signed another two year buyout last year. This is a rare situation, but being on a buyout for an in house film for, say, five years is more common.

I urge my students to audition for international projects as well and prepare them for the auditioning process. This is when your accent or other languages and any different looks comes in handy. Generally these projects require self tapes and call on special skills such as weapons, horsemanship, dance or combat training along with the accents or languages. Longer hair on guys and girls (as usually they play Vikings, natives, or old world roles where buzz cuts were not common) as well as physical fitness is also usually looked for in these audition calls.

Again, do not audition for an international project if you do not have an active passport. Do mention every language you speak on your resume. Always, always memorize your taped international auditions. When should you really memorize audition text for any film and commercial work? Whenever you humanly can, actually. Hold the text at all times, sure, if you need to, but it is a real professional who holds the text and does not need it, as opposed to putting the text down and not being memorized. Doing it right and looking confident gets you the job.

National Audition Calls

A word about large, very publicized national calls. These happen in two ways: large 'cattle calls' where you and thousands of others go to one location and stand in line for hours and many of you never get seen; or online national calls where you and thousands of others submit self tapes in the hopes of being cast. National calls are geared to *only* pick out the biggest, loudest, most gorgeous actors/singers who submit or show up. It is also very rare that anyone is discovered in a national call. I, as an actor, never did them as they took up too much of my time. You may choose to do them, but be aware of the fact that going to smaller auditions and meeting people will impact your career faster and more positively than national calls. Sending in self tapes to smaller and better organized auditions will also better use your self taping time as well. National calls are endless, tiring and can pound on your spirit when, after eight hours in line, you are glanced at for two seconds before they say, "Next!" If you choose to do them, stay positive and energized and do not let them wear you down.

7

THE AUDITION: VOICE OVERS, NARRATION, ANIME, ANIMATION, AUDIOBOOKS

What's up, Doc?

Mel Blanc, 'The Man of a Thousand Voices'

Perhaps you have been told by people many times that you have a gorgeous voice. That does not mean that you need to have a career in voice over, nor will this chapter teach you anything but the practical points. But you can have, if you want to, a voice over career without an agent. The voice over industry is drastically different from how it was twenty years ago, when you could barely get a foot in the door. With the explosion of audiobook work, and work voicing games and anime and animation, this is now a viable career option if you know what to do and how to do it. It is not, no matter how it may sound or appear, easy work. Voice work is much more than commercials and anime. Every time you get a recorded message on the phone or hear a voice in an elevator, these are all examples of voice work. Specific training is vital and the ability to be flexible vocally is as well. An additional talent is being able to engineer your own work at home.

One of the great rules about doing voice work is that it does not matter what your face looks like, even in an audition, which can be live, as long as you get the sound to come out that gets you the job. Especially if you self record at home in your own studio you can use tongue twisters or exercises to warm up, and listen to your self recording to hear if you are clear. Treat your voice as if it is precious, keep your throat hydrated, practise clarity and diction, and read aloud a lot. I mean a lot. Every day, in fact. You want to be able to sight read any and every word possible in the English language, including slang (whazzap!), foreign phrases (c'est la vie) and odd words (ubiquitous! solipsistic!) without a hitch.

Learning how to work with your breath is also an amazing and very needed talent. It brings a reality to your voice work that often gets you the job. It can not only help you read long passages without getting winded, but can be added and used in many ways to show emotion, a big audible sigh before, "Gosh, he was soooo cute!", can make your reading of the line stand out from everyone else who simply reads the line plainly (the same goes for other real sounds like squeals, giggles, stammers and more). Look for what is not in the written line and let us hear it. Voice work is much more than the words on the paper.

Voice Exercises: Find Your Four Main Voices

Exercises that can be done to start to work with your voice are to begin to find four voices that you can pull out of your hat at an audition without thinking about it. One you already have – it is your best, cleanest, normal clear voice. It sounds like you with a medium pace and very clear enunciation. That second one that you need to learn how to do on a moment's notice is one at the lower end of your vocal range. Talk your voice down slowly to the lower end of your range and find a lower area where you are not straining in any way, but you are still in a relaxed low speaking range. It needs to be low, but not the lowest you can go. It is still a voice you could work in for a few hours with no strain. That is voice number two and when you get an audition note, "Can you sound more powerful, older, authoritarian, professorial, smarter, eloquent, etc.", that is the voice you pull out of your toolbox. Voice number three is just like number two except it is in your high range and can be your 'cartoon' or anime or fun voice. Do not talk yourself all the way up into your highest range, just find a voice you can control that is high pitched and that you know you could use for an hour without killing your vocal cords. That is the 'sillier, cartoon-y, little kid, hyper, etc.' voice you can do when asked. The fourth voice is only two to three notes up from your normal, clean narrator voice and I call it the Barbie voice (or Ken voice for the boys). It is like your normal voice, but two or three notes higher and it is used when you read an audition and then someone says, "Can you do it again but be younger, brighter, cheerful, fun loving, more like a teen, etc.". Having these four different voices in your back pocket makes you able to say, "Sure, I can!", and do whatever type of sound you are asked for without minutes of mulling it over. In a voice audition you must be able to throw out voices and sounds within a rapid amount of time.

Another way to lock these, and other voices you find, into your head and thus into finding a home in your vocal cords is to work with images as you do voice work. Especially in audiobook work, where you may be required to come up with forty-five or more different voices for a book, across a spectrum of ages and genders, imagery can be a real helpful tool. For any voice you may have any problems finding or working with, get an image of someone you know, or an actor, an actor in a well known role, a character from a book, but an image in your mind of a person. Find an image that works for you to produce a voice when you think of that image. A voice student of mine had issues finding a voice for a book until I asked her to think of an image, a person or a character as I reread the role description to her. As I read the description of the role she thought and then said, "Oh, Lilith from *Frasier!*", and with that image it then brought forth a voice from her throat that she was able to work with.

A Voice Studio at Home

How to set up a recording studio in your home, rough-style. Pick a closet or any space that is small but big enough for you to record in (remembering your computer, microphones, text and a small table and maybe a chair should fit in there as well). Closets are favorites because there are already clothes hanging in them, which deadens sound. There are also no windows in closets. You want deadened and flat sounds, no echoes, no booming of your voice off walls. A closet or a small room with no windows is best. Amazon is well known for having affordable sound setups and I would refer any beginning voice actor to check the videos at ACX.com for the best home studio equipment recommendations.

Now most smart voice actors will try to develop an in home studio. There are numerous videos online on YouTube, which can instruct you in how to do this and all of the various equipment options there are for it in a varying price range. Thus, at home in your studio how do you begin to do takes of something to practise? Well, do not just jump in; make sure you have at least the basic setup for a headset with microphone and a recording and editing software (Audacity is a great free software). Play with the software, record short files and learn how it all works first.

Then prepare the text you have chosen, making sure it is something you like (especially when starting out, read things you like to read), and score it as a musician scores a piece of music (Where do I breathe? What different voice is this? What is that word in Russian that I need to circle or write out phonetically? Where does the tone change? Where does the argument start?). Do not overthink it, just score it instinctively. This helps you to be prepared before you record, with both your technical equipment and knowledge of how to use it, and with your text mapped out, whether in an engineering studio or in your house.

When recording for the first time, relax. Just begin calmly and in your best and cleanest voice (and by clean, I mean clear, in your most normal and workable range, with diction and enunciation) start to read. Your best and cleanest voice should also double as your main narrator voice for any audiobooks or narrative voice overs whenever possible. At least 50 to 60 percent or more of most books are narrator driven and thus the best choice is to use a clean and clear normal voice for the narrator and clear male (a few notes down from your normal voice) and female (a few notes up from your normal voice) choices for leading voices. You want to be able to read long pages without taxing your vocal cords. Also always keep in mind that you should read at least 5 to 10 percent slower than you want to. I actually tell my brain to be 20 percent slower than my normal speaking pace. You need that pace for listeners to follow what you say.

It is sometimes very difficult to work on long voice texts at home in your studio without some direction, which is why I teach my students different exercises for scoring texts. Mark in the text the breathing places, different voices, words that are bothersome or new to you, pronunciations, changes in book tone, when different accents come in. Separate out and score each scene as well (for instance, if you have a five page scene with six characters and they are arguing, be careful that you are sure of who exactly is speaking each line when and take the time in the reading to change clearly back and forth for each voice). Scoring also helps to set all the 'He said' and 'She commented' statements, so that you can flip back into your narrative voice from the character voices. Scoring gives you a complete roadmap of what and how to read, and it makes recording the text a whole lot easier.

Also, when you finally do sit down to record the audiobook, create a score mark (maybe an X is your mark) and mark it as you go when you have to do a 'restart'. A restart is when the line reads, "He walked down the street and as he peered over the tops of cars, he saw her." However, when you begin recording you say, "He walked down the street and as he peeped –" Do not repeat 'peeped', which is the word you flubbed. Go back to the beginning of that sentence (yes, the entire sentence) and restart the entire sentence. Do it in a relaxed manner, even if you restart it five times, as each restart should sound exactly the same. Take a big breath as you do, and also score your text with an X or some other sign or symbol where the restart begins. Do not panic over it or get annoyed (if you do, we can hear it clearly on the tape in your voice); take a deep breath as your eyes go back to your restarted sentence and say it again.

You mark the restarted sentence with an X because, if you are recording in a home studio, you do not want to have to listen to everything to find the four restarts you made that day. And if you are editing your own work it is much harder to pinpoint the millisecond between words to edit out the one word that you flubbed. If you are aiming to edit out half a sentence that was flubbed, it is much easier to find it and edit it. If you are recording in a professional studio and there are sound engineers working with you, they usually will catch these things and edit them out themselves, but they will still appreciate you noting your own restarts as well. This is one of the marks of a professional. You always want to be in control of the text, so do not let it control you.

Be aware for all your audio work that a listening ear is usually three to five words behind your speaking voice, listening and processing the words you say and the images you give voice to. Take your time. Seriously, read your audiobook text at least 20 percent slower than you speak normally. You can only change from voice to voice and be very clear if you take the time to do it. This is the one gripe in auditions about actors reading for voice work: in the beginning you will consistently read way too fast. As well, if you are not certain or have not been told what the gender of a role is (this can happen a lot), just pick a gender and go for it (especially in a live audition if you do not get a chance to ask). Just take your time above all else.

Voice Over Auditions

Voice over auditions can be both live or self tapes (for easier editing of self tapes, record the slate if asked for and each take as you do it, so you end up with one file with all takes on it, and use the pause button, as opposed to the stop button, when you record your takes). You should instinctively learn to recognize the brand name, the product and the taglines (Got Milk?) in your text. Often in a live voice audition you will read for the producer of the project, and may be cast then and there in the room, as they make all casting decisions. So, taglines and product names are key. These are important to the company who might hire you.

When you do work in sound booths, whether to audition for jobs or to record actual jobs, it really is a big difference from working in your little home studio in that you can just relax and act. You do not have to worry about editing or voice regulation or anything except your text, your headphones, the sound engineer outside who may or may not give you adjustments, the director outside who may or may not give you acting notes and even sometimes a video monitor you must watch to match your dialogue with someone you are dubbing (or an animated character you are voicing). Yep, you only have those things to worry about . . .

If, at any time in your early career, you can afford thirty minutes in a real sound studio do pay for it and record some clips. Use them in your demo reel. Get the experience of being in a recording studio and working with an engineer under your belt. My very first engineering booth audition was a revelation to me as I had never been in a sound booth before. It threw me very badly and I did not book the job. I stammered and stuttered and wrestled with the headphones. Learn from my mistake.

Additional Dialogue Recording

ADR is another lovely way to get into voice work. ADR (additional dialogue recording) can usually consist of dubbing (you can dub foreign voices or even mimic US actors if you sound like them) and the secondary ADR non-dialogue market is also growing, which is more sound based (like breathing, panting, martial arts sounds, screaming, laughing and more). You can prepare for all of these types of work and record clips of all of these and put them on your ninety second audio demo reel as well. Stamina should be worked on vocally so that you are able to stand or sit in an audio booth (as most ADR is done in an engineering studio) and pant for ten or fifteen minutes, or scream for the same amount of time (I know an ADR actress in Los Angeles who only does scream work and has fifteen separate types of screams in her 'toolbox' and listed on her resume, including 'scream with death gurgle', 'scream of teenager', 'scream of mom' and so forth).

ADR is also sitting or standing and making sounds as if you are punching someone and being punched for fifteen minutes or so, as martial arts and action films use those sounds a lot. Stamina and breath control are vital for this field, as is the ability to watch a monitor while you produce sounds to match the action shown there, but it is great fun to do this work. Where else can you pant and make karate sounds or laugh for ten minutes and make a great paycheck?

The smart voice actors I know also have both a commercial audio reel and a character audio reel. A character reel would do well to have not only different voices, ages, genders and such, but also accents and even languages. A French clip will not hurt a reel in 2018 – it will help. That is very different from ten years ago. As well, a good commercial reel would do even better if an audiobook clip is included within it. Many audiobook agencies now even look for foreign language readers who are based in the US for the French, Spanish and German markets.

Animation Voice Work

Anime and animation auditions can also be great fun and a few of the things that can help you create a voice on the spot are probably right there in the script itself. Look for age, gender, behavior and any other clues about character in the text (Do they stutter? Are they spoken about as being loud? What do others say about them? Are they called obnoxious?). You can ask at the audition if there is a visual idea of the role (they may pull out a drawing that then inspires you with a new voice). If you are the only actor in the entire auditions that day who asks that question about a visual idea then you may be the only actor who sees that character drawing. This also goes for video game voices. By the time video game roles are being actively auditioned for, they do have visual ideas for the roles and often can show you a drawing. If you are very lucky they may not only hire you, but redesign their drawings and pattern a video game role directly after you.

Room tone is something that is very different across all media types. Room tone is often used to refer to two or so seconds that are recommended to be at the beginning and end of any audio file you record in your home studio. This is also called giving a file a 'head and tail' and is also used in audiobook recording as well as any recorded auditions. Room tone on television or film sets is a bit different. At some point on a film or TV set you will hear the sound person say something like, "Everyone freeze for room tone." Then everyone will freeze in a comfortable position and the sound person will record up to ten minutes of the 'sound' of the room. Every room on a set, every location, has a unique sound all its own; the air in it and pipes or building sounds and so forth all give any room a special sound pattern. The room also sounds different with people in it and without people in it. Bodies absorb sound (this is why stage actors have to be louder on stage). Both kinds of room tones are things you will have to become very familiar with in your work.

Why record room tone in film or television? What the heck use is it? Well, let us say you just shot a great dramatic scene where you looked out the window and you were wonderful and emotional and angst filled. The light was perfect, the moment was stunning, your acting was Oscar worthy, but then faintly in the distance there was the sound of the 'blap-blap-blap' of a car alarm. Nevertheless you, the true professional, kept on emoting and the director kept on shooting. In the editing room the director can take some of that lovely room tone and put that in and remove the car horn sound and the scene is then perfection.

The rules for physical auditions described in the other chapters apply for voice auditions too. Voice actors are actors; they just usually do not appear on film. But any of the tips in this book for film auditions will help a voice actor as well. It is all about the text and acting choices, whether you use your voice only or not. The trend will continue to grow, however, for both voice and other actors to self tape and self record for auditions. There is also a very large market for 'sound alikes', people who can impersonate well known voices or manipulate their voice to sound like the voice of someone else, or even like older cartoon characters. Often the hiring of a sound alike or person to do the voice match is required because a celebrity is either unavailable or too expensive to hire. However, be certain that all the legalities are followed and that your representation of the voice is marketed as a parody or satire or is cleared legally. If it is not cleared then you could be involved in some possible legal action if the spot is passed off to the public as the real celebrity voice.

Audiobooks and Accent Work

Working as a freelancer on audiobook work can be done by auditioning via a variety of sites online such as ACX and Findaway, but you must be very ready vocally, have an extraordinary ability to read and perform text without it feeling like you are 'reading' it, have an audio reel or two and many different audio clips, and also be especially technically savvy enough to do the engineering end of the work. Take a class in voice work or even study privately with someone like me who has done audiobooks and can not only help you to learn how to deal with many types of text and dialogue, genre and tone as an actor, but who also can help you learn the rough ropes of the home studio set up and about the pre and post recording engineering processes. This is often a great way to pay your bills while you can and then use your other time to make films, write, act, etc. However, you must study audiobook work so that you do it correctly.

A section of the audiobook market is still untapped and that is the market for actors who are adept at accents. In a physical audition for a role you can get away with a 'gloss' of an accent (a gloss, again, is what I call it when you do just enough of an accent and it lets me know that if cast you could work with an accent coach and get it right). In audio work my casting preference is that your accents are perfect and you either do the accent right at the audition or do not attempt it at all. As well, do not have accents on your voice reel if they are not absolutely impeccable. That will cost you work.

What if you have an accent yourself as an actor? Should you lose it? If it is an accent that you feel is keeping you boxed into certain types of roles, or you feel is holding you back, then yes, you may want to find a good coach and begin to lose it. Or do not try to lose it, but change it a bit. Keep in mind that 'losing' an accent fully takes years and years and may involve great emotional and mental pain in that process, as there are familial, cultural and personal associations that go along with that accent. When it seems to be the case that you cannot unlearn your natural accent completely, then you can begin to learn instead how to do a standard American accent. Often times I will simply teach a foreign student to do an American accent instead of having them lose the accent they have if the one they have is very marketable.

If you want to learn accents, as well, get an accent or dialect coach. If you can, get an accent coach who has worked in both film and stage (as I have). Why? Because there is a big difference between doing a perfect Irish accent in real life and then doing one that can be understood when you do it on stage, and one that can be understood when you do it in a film. There is a difference in how an actor carries an accent and attitude on a stage and in a film. Get an accent coach who understands that. You do not want to be doing a perfect Basque accent that simply cannot be understood in an audition; you want to be doing a beautiful Basque accent that we love, yet still understand for the film.

How do you begin to work with dialogue, voices, pitches, breathing, genres in voice work? You begin by listening, reading and noticing the sounds around you. There are so many great books and courses that you can get information from and there are exercises you can do at home to help increase your casting power. Read all the time, act the books out, learn to love and read words, grow your vocabulary daily and make it beyond huge, learn how to take a deep breath (I call it silent breathing) without making a sound on tape. The trick is to inhale through the mouth, nose and throat all at the same time, but silently, and fill your lungs completely. Practise it so that you can record yourself doing it and never hear it. Pay attention to genres even on TV – how does the vocal feel change if it is a sci-fi show? How is that different from a romance? How does a western sound? How can you embody that genre and emotion in your voice?

Emerging Technology You May Compete Against

Vocaloids are an emerging technology rich invention that may eventually change the voice world, and may even be your competition. Certainly they are already changing backup and jingle singing and are drifting into popular music now as lead singers. Songs such as "Hirari, Hirari" by Kito are quite popular, and Kito is a vocaloid. A vocaloid is a synthesized singing voice and many of them are very close to being indistinguishable from a human voice. In the programming of vocaloids one can also insert vibrato and the inhalation of breaths. We have only begun to assess what they may mean for the singing industry and whether they will take work away from real singing voices. Their application in spoken word is just beginning to be played with and there is a slight possibility, at least in Japan and Spain where they are very popular, that they may capture a small corner of the voice acting market. They are finding a third market in the US and within ten years they could easily have a small percentage of the US market of vocal work as well. I do not see that happening, as there is usually an inherent sound difference and emotional timbre in the human voice that is loved and preferred for audiobook work, but I may be wrong.

Another way voice work is very different now from how it was twenty years ago is that, if you speak languages other than English, you can now find work in those languages while still living in the United States. You can do audiobooks in various languages now while living in the United States and that was not the case ten to fifteen years ago. Many casting agents actively are looking for actors who read in languages other than English. Many TV shows also need languages and are filmed in the US and Canada, as are many anime shows.

Smart voice actors all have small snippets of audiobooks in their voice reel, which can be even up to a few minutes long. Audiobooks are also being recorded in many different languages now so make use of this and include your languages on your resume as well as on your reel. If you are bilingual or quadrilingual there is no reason in the world to not show it on an acting reel and a voice reel. Do not limit yourself in any way, show off all of your talents.

Voice Work Trends to Come

The voice work trend that I predict will grow is the precasting of voice work without auditions. Now, often voice over actors are found online and cast, or cast because they were recommended for work by agents. This may eliminate general auditions for voice work in the future. There will be a trend of speedier deadlines of days or hours depending upon the voice project, a trend of smaller in home studios where voice actors are working with laptops and software (as I do), and an absolutely massive continued growth of the audiobook market internationally. Get in on the ground floor and use that talented voice you have.

8

THE AUDITION: ALL THE NEW MEDIA

I believe the hardest challenge actors have isn't talent, isn't craft, isn't discipline, but issues of self-esteem lack, fear and DOUBT.

C. Stephen Foster

The audition styles you never get prepared for are the ones that you will miss out on as they may not even be on your radar. If they are not on your radar, you may then become afraid of them over time and never work up the nerve to audition. No matter what on-camera class you take you usually will not study found footage auditions, short-form content for Hulu or Amazon Prime auditions, motion capture performance and audition prep, blue and green screen work and how to prepare for these at home, or how to go through callbacks for all of the above. However, you can be more than ready for all these things. Much of new media often starts out as non-union work, and you can get in on the ground floor then. The path to work becoming union sanctioned, paid and produced is becoming shorter with every successful project that comes to fruition. You want to get in on the ground floor.

Specialty Auditions in Any Media

You may, as an artist, encounter what I call 'specialty' auditions. These have been much more prevalent in the past, and hopefully some will not be as popular now. By that, I mean the one specialty I hope ends: where you as an able bodied actor are called in to audition for a role that has cerebral palsy or a serious disability. Hopefully actors with those disabilities will now be called in more to audition for them, but what happens if you are called in to audition instead? Well, short of turning down the role and demanding that they call in a disabled artist (which they might or might not then do), you can do the research and at least be responsible for recognizing and reflecting what it is you are auditioning for. Understand the disability, do your research and present it correctly, not as a caricature. Often a casting person may have no idea what a person with cerebral palsy may present in behavior (this is part of the reason they may be fearful of bringing in an actor with it, which is a huge fault of the casting person), so you need to be the one who presents the truth.

This also goes for auditions where you have to act a role with a speech impediment (understand then what the impediment actually is and reproduce it truthfully) or something along the lines of a bipolar disorder. Do not show up with a generalized audition, or something that mocks the condition; be very specific and understand what the disability is. Whether or not the role is written accurately is not your worry, unfortunately, and you cannot control whom they cast, but auditioning truthfully and specifically will help the overall disability representation in the visual media if you are cast in the role. If you are not cast in the role you may still teach someone a truth about it. Hopefully the future will see more and more wonderful disabled artists cast in these roles and in non-disabled roles as well.

Other types of specialty auditions may require you to act as if you are drunk or high on a variety of drugs. Simple tip for being drunk: most drunks act very specifically as if they are *not* drunk. They get louder, more pointed in their speech and use their hands more. These three small tips are usable for being 'drunk' in an audition. Again, do your research about alcohol and whatever drug you are supposed to be on. It does you no good to assume a certain drug makes you slow and mellow, but not to really know that the drug you are addicted to in the film or play is one that makes you very hyperactive. There should never be any assumptions with any type of specialty audition; do your research just as you would with any other audition. Actors who research get the roles, period.

As well as research, let me say again, it will grow annoying, but seriously. Have a dictionary app on your phone – I cannot say that enough. iPhones and any phone with internet are a godsend not only for the dictionary apps, but also to look up the young filmmaker you are auditioning for or to refresh the last project the casting director cast. You can check unions (and union auditions, benefits or special notices once you are union) on your phone as well as any casting apps. Make use of the technology. There is no excuse anymore to not be fully prepared. Actors who say, "Oh, I only have an email", will find it hard to get work. I only know one actor with no web presence at all who works a lot in New York City and that is due to his immense talent and his sterling reputation (and he recites in Greek, talk about language skills!).

Speaking of technology, prepare yourself when you walk into any audition room. There are all kinds of cameras that may be in there, everything from a huge 'on set' camera to a lone guy with an iPhone – or perhaps someone will be attached to a steadicam moving around you as you audition. What they have in the room is what they will use that day and you should have your mind well prepared to act for any and all cameras you ever encounter, as well as any number of people. The key is knowing your own face and how it works with the camera. If you do not know your own face you will not find it easy to work in film and especially not in motion capture or green screen.

Green Screen Work

Often on a green screen set, if the entire film is a green screen film, you will work in an entirely green room and you may not ever move at all. I have worked on green screen films where the actors acted like they were walking, but did not, as the passing of houses or scenery would be added in later. Your 'camera choreography' may then need to be very small, nonexistent, or micro-directed. By micro-directed I mean that you may be instructed to move your hand two inches left on this line, and you need to be able to be that precise. You can also practise this at home, and I certainly would if I knew I had a blue or green screen audition.

Green Screen Practice Exercise

Working with this technology requires you to be able to not only be artistic, but very technical and precise yourself. Since a great deal of things are added with CGI you can do numerous exercises at home where you act with nothing, or with inanimate objects, or with your pet. Read a scene with nothing but air; however, place a piece of tape on the wall opposite you, up high, and make your scene partner a ten foot tall dragon. Not only must you act your own role, but you must imagine your partner's reaction to you and then react to that imagined reaction. If you can react to a partner who is not there, having reactions they do not have because they do not exist, you will captivate us. We may even look over to where you are acting to check if something is really there! Use your imagination, as any exercise of this nature is beneficial, so that when you are faced with an audition you do not overdo the acting or energy or reactions too much.

The day you walk into a blue screen or green screen set for callbacks or to act in a film is quite something. The set itself, if it is a complete green screen film, will be completely neon green floors, ceiling, walls – everything a neon (and let me say 'neon' again) and bright green. In fact, after three to five straight hours working on a green screen set, you may want to have Advil and water in your actor bag as your eyes and head will be exhausted simply from working in the constant glaring green.

Found Footage Auditions

Then there are the found footage auditions. Found footage films (*The Blair Witch Project* is the originator of this genre) generally end up being horror films and they often base the roles on the actual actors they hire, so your ability to be real and also improvise dialogue is essential. There is a technique for found footage auditions (largely these films begin with no text or script in hand and they write it as it is first fully improvised, using your own improvisation as the actual text), as usually they are all improvisation in the auditions. These films always feel as if they are real life and just happened to be filmed. Thus, usually one of the secrets in the audition is that you are filmed from the moment you enter the audition room, not from when the filming starts and they say 'action'. Most likely the director or producer will set up a scene and ask you to improvise that scene with them.

What are they really looking for in these films that begin with no script? A relaxed and real actor who can let emotions and dialogue flow. But, what actual emotions? As most found footage films are horror films, the emotions most sought after are anger, fear and grief. If you can work these into your improvised found footage audition you will do well. Then the callbacks are usually group improvisations and are much more to gauge the chemistry among the main three or four actors. Callbacks are about all of the above emotions as well as your individual chemistry within the group of three or four actors.

Blue Screen Work

What is blue screen? Roughly, it can be used to add to or take away from the film. Think of the film *Forrest Gump* and Captain Dan's legs. Removing Gary Sinise's legs, after the character lost his, is an example of blue screen technology. Gary Sinise wore blue stockings from the kneecaps down and the computer removed anything that color from the film scene and replaced it with the background images. If you are in a blue screen shoot and wearing a blue glove to your elbow, but then lose your focus or your technical grasp and put your prop in that same hand, you have blown it, as on playback we then see a floating prop. Prepare so these little things do not blow the job for you.

Green screen can be almost the opposite to blue screen as roughly, it adds additional images into the film as its primary focus, rather than removing them. You have seen the numerous science fiction films where the city of New York lies in ruins. They have just added computer generated images in where they put up a green screen. However, how do you audition for these types of films? First, understand that in both a blue or green screen audition and performance you may very well be acting with empty air. But you will be acting, and usually will not even see any screen until callbacks or much later on the set. Acting with imaginary things does not mean acting harder or bigger; it actually means continuing to be real and even more specifically focused on where those things are.

A great tip for green or blue screen work is to close your eyes between takes on the set. Or even slap on sunglasses between takes. Do not wear *any* shade of blue shirt to a blue screen audition or filming and, of course, do not wear *any* shade of green to a green screen audition or filming.

Motion Capture

The use of photogrammetric facial capture and motion capture is growing at an enormous rate; however, how can you train for a motion capture audition or career? There is the WETA Digital in New Zealand, Mocap Academy in London, Captivate Action Ltd. in London and Australia, and the newly created Mobile Motion in Los Angeles. Note there are many places that film motion capture work, but not very many that train actors for it. Training in New Zealand and England is optimal as that is where it all started, and where the greats of motion capture like Andy Serkis or Terry Notary got their training. Motion capture is used in film (Gollum in *Lord of the Rings*) and in many video games (*Near Dark*, for example) and even in TV series and commercial work. Thus, motion capture auditions are usually heavily physical, or dance and movement based, and casting directors are on the lookout for athletes, gymnasts and actors with dance backgrounds (as probably you will be playing an animal, alien or something with a lot of physical movement). That does not mean that an average actor cannot do motion capture, nope. Stamina is often more important than athletics in motion capture work, so if you have stamina it will often get you work.

The emphasis in motion capture is on body type and body control. (Imagine doing a take of you, playing an alien, crawling through an alien landscape, up a hill and over the bodies of your comrades. You will do that on a life size set. Now do that take twenty more times with exactly the same physicality as you just did it. Stamina.) Facial acting is often secondary, though still important (Andy Serkis, perhaps the best known actor of motion capture, is also a brilliant actor). Physical awareness is vital as well, so that you don't whip your head around or touch your face in a motion capture setting. Oscar winner Lupita Nyong'o has funny stories of her work in *Star Wars: The Force Awakens* and how many times she actually ate the markers off of her face by touching them accidentally and brushing them into her mouth.

Motion capture work often blossoms out of an actor doing very good voice work on a project. Casting directors for voice gigs for animated series or video games often may be the very same people who cast actors for motion capture work. If they do not cast for it they are often asked about voice actors by those who do cast for video-game motion capture. This trend of voice actors being recruited for video game or other motion capture work is another trend that I predict will grow.

Be real with motion capture, but also be calculated with your facial work in auditions for motion capture. There may also be, unlike in most casting situations, more than one actor cast in the very same role in motion capture work as perhaps you can act very well and also climb trees, but they then need someone to do backflips and jump through eight hoops of fire and that is not within your talent or athletics range. Then a stunt person may also play the role for the very complicated physical parts, so there may be three of you in the same role.

Video Game Motion Capture

In doing video game motion capture you will tend to have fewer 'markers' (those little dots) than for a feature film, maybe forty-five or fifty on your entire body. In a feature film you may have fifty to 100 markers on your face alone. Where and how many markers are set on you in your skin tight suit will tell you the focus of the project, body or face. In situations like *The Hobbit* or anything with Andy Serkis, you will see upwards of 500 to 1,000 or more markers on every part of his face and body as they track every single aspect of his performance. This issue may all be outdated in two years or so as now marker-less motion capture is in full research and development by a variety of companies and does seem achievable. The company that works it out will become an industry powerhouse. If it does come to fruition then actors will not need to understand how to work with markers (not touching, dislodging or blocking them) any longer and it will be even easier to audition and book work in the motion capture industry.

The Sawmill in California is one of the many new places in the United States where some motion capture work is done and where young actors can work and enter this aspect of the business. They have a great website with information about motion capture that is practical and professional, such as keeping all hair back from your face for a motion capture session (and indeed for any motion capture audition) as well as close fitting clothing needing to be worn. All their tips are great for auditions as well. Keep your eye on The Sawmill, as they are going places, and I highly recommend training with them if you can. The motion capture industry has not even begun to fulfil its potential so get any training to get your foot in this door.

9

AUDITIONS FOR STAGE AND WITH SHAKESPEARE OR VERSE PLAYS

You know it. Don't think about it as Shakespeare, just let it be real. Breathe.

Anthony Sher, during his time at the Royal Shakespeare Company

Shakespeare and other 'heightened language' plays not only are something you should audition for to stretch your acting and articulation muscles, but also for the added benefit of learning how to work with period text, science fiction text, old English text, complicated text, and heightened text in general. I also always recommend auditioning for anything, whether it be Shakespeare or not, that scares you or makes you a bit nervous. Any audition or role that makes you fearful you should always go for, or why are you acting? Embrace the challenge. If you are scared then that means that the job will teach you something and, if you want a career that is competitive, you must always be learning and adapting and challenging yourself.

Take your time in any work with heightened language as well. Usually in auditions the call goes out for an actor within a ten year age range and then the auditions are held. I oddly was involved once in an audition call where instead of posting a ten year age range (as is the accepted norm) they mistakenly posted a twenty year age range. So we found ourselves seeing men from twenty five to forty five years old. This was a project with heightened language and we must have seen about twenty or so young men all in their mid-twenties in a row. A few were very talented, but all were at a fast pace that was nervous and a bit rushed, really because of the language. Then a man came in who was in his early forties. He took his time with the thoughts, the beats, the heightened dialogue, and the entire room visibly relaxed and exhaled. This was a professional who took his time about thinking and acting (while using the text at a relaxed and nimble pace) and this was the fellow who got cast.

There is a wonderful and often fresh approach to Shakespeare plays every day in every city in the US. Experimentation with setting, period, tempo and dress is never ending. However, I still have to sit through auditions where everyone reads Shakespeare as if they are on *Downton Abbey*. Any actor can and should read in an absolutely normal voice; you are not required to become instantly British. Or loud. Or to overact. That is an acting stereotype. However, those actors new to Shakespeare I do invite to go to YouTube where they should view anything with Mark Rylance, arguably the finest Shakespearean actor alive today, in it. He treats the text as if he were speaking it in a modern day setting, talking as matter-of-factly as we all do in the present day. He happens to be British, but I venture that if he were not then he might not do it in a British accent.

Acting and Auditioning Shakespeare

Shakespeare is not to be treated as 'precious' and does not need to be pontificated. It should be read at a quick pace, as normal people speak nowadays. Women, you also do not need to wear a floor length dress to a Shakespeare audition. If you are comfortable with the text it will not matter if you wear jeans and a t-shirt. This is a change from acting Shakespeare ten or fifteen years ago, where treating the words as precious, especially in the US, was the accepted norm and was even encouraged by many acting companies. Thanks to actors like Mark Rylance and many, many educators and producers, the 'take' on Shakespeare is changing and becoming much more realistic. When it was performed in Shakespeare's time it was realistic and quick or the audience got bored. Be aware that can happen in auditions today too.

Nothing is more disturbing in an audition than for me to speak to an engaging and interesting actor with an American accent and then to have them suddenly open their mouth to audition and exclaim, "TO BE OR NOT TO BEEEE!", overly dramatically and in a heavy

British accent. Wow. Where did the interesting actor go? An audition like that does not reveal the actual actor to me at all and it also lets me know that the actor is still caught up in a stereotype of Shakespearean acting. Usually I might not hire that actor, not because they have no talent, but because a rehearsal process is not where I should have to teach actors how to act Shakespearean text. I want actors who already come to rehearsal ready to play. If I do cast that very good actor who needs a bit of work I will often cast them in a smaller role knowing I can work with them on that.

Another thing that can be sometimes very disturbing and very boring when casting a Shakespeare play is when I see fifteen actors do the exact same speech in roughly the same way at the audition. There are many wonderful smaller and very rarely done speeches in Shakespeare. Search them out and do those, as that alone may get you noticed. Make use of the greatest modern tool for actors, the internet. Search there for little known monologues from Shakespeare's plays (or other writers of that same time period) and stun us with something rarely seen. Switch genders and do a monologue of the opposite sex for us – again, shake it up. Surprise us.

Shakespearean Text Exercise 1

Shakespeare scares many actors so let's talk about a few easy exercises to get you moving with this heightened text. Pick a Shakespearean monologue – a short one is best as most auditions will only ask for a one to two minute monologue anyway. Line by line, write out a paraphrase of it (exactly like the paraphrasing of a song exercise in this book), what it means to you in your own words, in modern day English. If you normally use slang, use it in your paraphrasing as well. Be aware when paraphrasing of any physical clues the text gives ("I hold this sword", for instance). Look up *every word* you do not know and translate it all into 'your' everyday speech. Then read them side by side so that, when you do actually perform the Shakespeare, not only do you know what you are saying, but it is in your own words, in your own body and in your own head. This will give a personal and real feel to your audition. Also, send thyself hence to *No Fear Shakespeare* (the link is in the resources section of this book) for modern translations of the text to help you out. The modern day

translations can help a lot, but really what helps the most is you trans-
lating it into *your* words. Then you own it.

Shakespearean Text Exercise 2

Another exercise that can help break your mind out of any preconceived notions about acting Shakespeare is to memorize whatever
Shakespearean text you are working on and then give yourself a very
large and involved physical activity. Shovel the snow in your driveway
while doing your monologue, chop wood for a fire while doing it,
go on a massive uphill hike, do an entire workout while doing the
monologue over and over. What purpose does this serve? It gets you
out of your head and back into your body. Shakespeare is often
seemingly acted from the neck up, and it is treated as if it is all about
the text and diction. However, in Shakespeare's day they were literally
all over the stage and it was very physically active, very bawdy. The
audiences ate meals and drank ale during the shows, so the actors had
to be fast, loud and physically exciting. If not they would get food
thrown at them from the audience. That is why 'downstage' is near
the audience, as the food would roll 'downstage' when it was thrown
at the actors. Thus, you must get the text out of your head and into
your body physically and you will start to get what chunks of it really
mean and how they work for your audition. Acting from the neck up
is never a good choice, whether speaking Shakespearean English or
modern day science fiction TV dialogue. Get your body involved.

Words, Words and More Words

For any kind of acting, but more so for stage or heightened language,
you must understand words. Try this tongue twister. Quickly.

> If a Hottentot taught a Hottentot tot to talk
> Ere the tot could totter,
> Ought the Hottentot tot be taught to say ought or naught,
> Or what ought to be taught 'er?

Do you know every word in it? Hottentot? Ere? Ought? Naught?
I have a twelve year old student who does, and knew it all correctly

on the very first read of it, so you should too. Or try this next poem on for size:

> I take it you already know Of tough and bough and cough and dough?
>
> Others may stumble but not you. Or hiccough, thorough, laugh and through?
>
> Well done: And now you wish perhaps To learn of these familiar traps:
>
> Beware of heard a dreadful word, That looks like beard and sounds like bird.
>
> And dead: It's said like bed, not bead, For goodness' sake, don't call it deed!
>
> Watch out for meat and great and threat, They rhyme with suite and straight and debt.
>
> A moth is not a moth in mother, Nor both in bother, broth in brother.
>
> And here is not a match for there Nor dear and fear for bear and pear
>
> And then there's does and rose and lose, Just look them up; and goose and choose.
>
> And cork and work and hard and ward And font and front and word and sword.
>
> And do and go and thwart and part – Come, come, I've hardly made a start!
>
> A dreadful language? Man alive, I'd mastered it when I was five!

If you cannot get through that poem cleanly pronouncing every single word correctly then check every word. Any word you are not 100 percent sure of, check it and learn it. Learn words, I cannot say it enough, but especially for stage and heightened language work.

Cold Reading Shakespeare

How can you read Shakespeare cold and still be stunning? First, as all of his plays are already published and pretty good to read, there is no real reason to ever read a scene cold in Shakespeare as you should at least recognize the play. However, I have an exercise I do with students who are often intimidated by Shakespearean text. I take a monologue and have them read it cold. They focus all their energy in how to act it and emote and they get stressed out sometimes. It usually is not very good, but that is fine. Then I have them take a deep breath, relax, and forget about acting any of it, and I have them simply read the text for punctuation *only*, no acting thoughts allowed at all. The goal is not to act, not to make sense of the text at all, simply to read the words and stop when there is a period or colon, pause when there is a comma or semicolon, ask a question when there is a question mark and so forth. The goal is to trust the text. The difference in the two readings is stunning.

By taking the pressure to 'act' away and just trusting the text (I mean, it is Shakespeare. You can trust this text to work) and simply reading the text for punctuation I see a dramatic shift in the monologue and the students' grasp of reading it. They see and feel the shift as well. They immediately start to understand it; they feel the difference of pace and the words themselves; they begin to get a glimmer of the love of the Bard, and then we are on the road to really working with Shakespearean text. Try the exercise yourself. I guarantee it will help you with understanding and feeling the text.

How Can Shakespeare Help You Work in a Digital World?

Learning how to deal with any 'heightened' text is also why working with Shakespeare can help get you that science fiction movie role or period piece role. Heightened language is also used in film and TV and in various web series all the time. Vocabulary, diction and language are really key to you getting cast as a cool new alien commander on that new TV show. If you cannot read, and especially cold read words well, you cannot get cast often unless you are very lucky. Diction and enunciation are also vital. Learn to speak so that you can be understood or you will audition and audition repeatedly and simply not get the work. Again, get a dictionary app and put it on your phone. (Have I said that enough, yet?) Read aloud.

Respect for film and stage history can actually get you more parts if you truly know your field. You have to know enough of plays (and yes, Shakespeare), screenplays and films to be able to understand cultural and cinematic or stage references. Those references pop up in all types of scripts and screenplays and if you do not get why your character keeps talking about feeling like he/she is in a Tennessee Williams play then you will have a hard time convincing me to cast you in that role. If I tell you that the screenplay you are reading for is roughly based on *Othello*, you should know what that means and you should have already read that play. Do you know the term 'Brechtian'? You should. Is someone's film inspired by Hitchcock? You should not only know who that is, but what that means in terms of cinematic reference and your acting of it. Any play or screenplay is about what the characters want and how they go about getting it, even Shakespeare or Brecht. Do not let yourself shy away from Shakespeare or any other old film, cultural reference or script.

For any stage auditions that are not involved with heightened language, you must still have impeccable diction and be good enough and professional enough with speech that we see you will be great in this role after a rehearsal period. Unlike in film, you do not have to 'match' the role as perfectly when you walk in. With stage auditions we know you will metamorphosize into the role if we see certain key things in your first audition. Even for children's theater auditions or musical theater auditions we still need to see those same things. What are those things? Clear and specific acting choices, a sense of volume (stage volume and film volume again are very different) and diction, physical presence and charisma (charisma is all about being yourself, your best and most interesting self, and very often this alone can get you cast), the ability to listen and to take notes, the ability to read and give and take with other actors you may work with. Hmm, and yes, of course, some talent never hurts.

10

THE CALLBACK. THE COLD READ. THE SCREEN TEST. IMPROVISATION

Don't try to be funny when you're being funny. If you try to be funny then you aren't funny.

Jack Klugman, actor

What could be better for any actor than getting a callback? Of course, getting the role. However there is also something in film and TV called being 'on hold' or 'on spec' for a part. It is directly in the middle of these two things. It is almost like you have the job, but not quite. 'On hold' can mean that the job or project is not fully set yet or the producers do not know if they want you or someone else to play the role. It could mean they are thinking of you for another role entirely or that they are reviewing your film audition to see if they think you could work well with another actor who is already cast. It means that they want you to wait, to be on hold, while they think it over and figure it out. It also means you do not take any other jobs while they decide about casting you.

Being 'On Hold'

Whether or not you are put on hold for a role is up to you (and your agent if you have one). If you are put on hold it is technically time that could be spent auditioning, booking and working on something else, so keep that in mind while considering the project that you are being put on hold for. If you are on hold, make sure it is a project that is worth it. Make sure it is for something you really want, something paying, something union (if you are wanting to become union) as you could lose other important work while waiting.

Callbacks

What then do callbacks really mean for an actor? They mean that we like you a lot as an actor, and we know you can act or sing or dance or all three. What we do not know is what your chemistry with other actors is like. There may be actors that have been precast and we need to see how you read with them, as well as with other actors we called back. If it is a stage play callback we may ask you to read the entire script before the callback. We also need another chance to get to know you, as you the person, to see if any red flags pop up for us (Are you high maintenance? Do you click with the other actors? Do you snap at the stage manager? Are you loud and obnoxious?) and whether you can take direction. Can you listen and communicate back to us well? What are you really like, so that we know how you will be to work with in rehearsal and on the set or stage.

Be aware that callbacks are about *far more* than the acting. I have seen countless actors blow a callback by being snarky, high maintenance, short with the stage manager, rolling their eyes at another actor (who happens to be the one who is precast) and so on. Build your reputation at a callback and build it with everyone from the production assistants to the prop person to the director. Also be aware of any intimacy in both auditions or callbacks. In an audition or callback you can and should ignore intimate stage directions, unless it is specifically discussed by the director, and *do not* make up any new ones. I once was precast in a role and the search was on for a male actor to star opposite me in this three person show. We narrowed the field to about a dozen fellows to come in and read with me and one of them was a very lovely actor with gorgeous eyes. He was a good actor when reading; however, at one point in the scene he leaned over and put his hand on my breast. Hmm. In discussing this later, the director (a woman) and I both were put off by that. As it was not in the text it was not needed (and as he was a gay man I did not think he was copping a free feel). However even if it had been in the text you would never do it in an audition or a callback unless it had been discussed and planned ahead. He did not get the role.

However, it was not the issue of that contact that lost him the part. In fact, making physical contact in an audition or a callback can nab you the role if done right. The issue with that particular situation was that he did not make the right kind of contact. In another very different audition I was again precast in a role and we auditioned many young men to play opposite me in a two person show. The director liked a very handsome young man who was a good actor and I had clicked with a different young man who had touched my hand with the right feel of connection. He had a different vibe from the obvious vibe for the role, but we clicked. We had a chemistry and instant trust and that is the actor who eventually was cast.

The issue in the first story was that it was a sexual type of contact that had not been discussed before reading the scene. However, fully 90 percent of actors never make any type of physical contact in any audition or callback. The type of physical contact I am talking about is very different and not sexual and every time I have been able to use it as an actor I got a callback or was cast; every time I hear from a student who has used it he or she has just been cast because of it. Darcy, one of my youngest students, Skyped me to tell me that she had gotten cast in *A Little Night Music* and that she knew the defining moment in her audition was when she reached out and touched the hand of the woman auditioning for her mother. She knew, she heard an audible gasp from the casting person when she touched her mother's hand, and she booked the role. It is a real touch and emphasizes the relationship with the other role. Try it.

The Magic Touch

What is this magic contact? First, it is not overtly sexual in any way and is not even really that big a deal, but it is a very specific and well thought out choice to touch the other actor or the reader at some point in the audition or callback scene. The touch may be a pat on the hand, touching their face, a slug on the shoulder – it is *very* specifically about who that role is in relation to yours and how you touch them because of that. Is it your boyfriend, mom, dad in the scene with you? Each touch is very different and very specific. The touch is about an honest human connection. After I have seen twenty actors read the same father–son scene and not move at all, and

I then see a smart young actor gently reach out and pat his 'dad' on the shoulder, I perk up. So does every casting director I know. I have just witnessed an honest moment of connection and this makes me cast the actors.

How many callbacks do you think is normal? For some Broadway musicals you may have eight or more callbacks. You may have four or five for a major movie role. However, usually no more than one or two. Callbacks are also a vital tool in your self assessment of how you are doing as an actor. If you have had three callbacks in the past month then you are on the right track to booking a gig. If you have had no callbacks within a year then you may need to think about seeing an audition coach or taking an audition prep class.

Screen Tests

Screen tests bring back thoughts of 1940s films, but they still happen in both films and TV. If you are brought in for a screen test it will probably be the same scene or scenes you have already read both in the auditions and callbacks. It still may not mean you get the role, however. The differences in screen testing from callbacks are that they then add in costumes, makeup and other actors, and then they film it. They may do three or four different looks with various hairstyles and costumes and makeup and you may do the scene with a very well known actor (and yes it must be memorized). They are testing not only the look and clothing, but also your chemistry with the other actors on the set. Be a professional and you'll get it.

Stage directions are very different in callbacks and screen tests from auditions. We have discussed the famous finger gun or the stabbing action (in Chapter 5) and why you do not want to ever pull that out in an audition. You may encounter a dramatic text, and the callback is the place to ask them (if they give you that same scene to read), "Should I mime shooting him this time?" They may say yes or no or even pull out a prop gun that you can use. Callbacks, however, are always the right place to ask about the stage directions. In screen tests you will always have the props.

The Improvisation Trend

A growing trend in film auditions and their callbacks is actors being asked to improvise either for an entire scene/situation or as an add-on (after the text in a scene is done, you may be asked to improvise as if the scene continues while the camera continues to film). If you do not know how to improvise I advise you to take a class very soon, as it is a growing trend and many times lines in a film or even a new play will change because you improvised something they like better. Any basics of improvisation you can learn in a good class; however, there are two great rules about improvising. The first is that, in any group improvisation setting (and a group is more than two people), be the first or second person into the scene or dialogue because then you have more control over what it is about. If four people are asked to improvise a scene and you are the last one to get involved you will mostly have to go along with whatever they have started. This is not good, as then you do not stand out and do not control what the improvisation is about. Instead, be the one who jumps in and starts the improvisation.

The second great rule about improvising is that, if you have any unusual or cool talent and have not been able to show that to the casting people thus far, bring it into the improvisation. Maybe you know they would just love your Russian accent. Bring it into the improvised scene. Jason Momoa booked the role of Khal Drago on *Game of Thrones*' not only because he could act and looked great for the role, but because he asked them (in a moment of brilliant improvisation) if he could show them a Haka, which is a traditional Maori war dance. Hakas are amazing and gorgeous and frightening and that is what put his audition over the top. His improvised idea and that Haka got him the role.

One of the best pieces of advice for callbacks is the same advice for the audition. Take your time. Good actors know the value of taking time, being a clear and clean reader and making the right choices on your feet. If you are rushing headlong through the text you can do none of this. The callback is truly the place to relax and embody the role. It usually is between you and a few others, not the hundreds of actors at the first audition. Own it in the callback, act as if the role is already yours. While you are in that room reading that role at the callback, nobody else in the world is reading it so it is yours for that moment in time. Own it and enjoy it.

Vocabulary Again? Yep

How knowing vocabulary can get you the part and why I keep yammering on about it. For the love of all the script gods, have a good vocabulary, have a dictionary app on your phone and pronounce words right. I went through an audition once for a leading role (a rare time in my auditioning life where you could actually hear all the other actresses auditioning) and the scene had the word 'episcopal' in it. (Put this book down and go look it up and memorize it if you do not know how to say it.) I actually listened to maybe twenty actresses audition and pronounce it 'epis-CO-pal' because the very first actress auditioning pronounced it that way, incorrectly. I was the very last actress to read; I pronounced it right and I got the part. Granted, I could act too, but the director told me weeks later that she was disappointed in seeing so many actors with no vocabulary knowledge until I said it correctly. Know the words. Know lots of words. Learn more words, every day. Learn trivia about words, learn slang. Learn heteronyms, synonyms and antonyms. Words are your life as an actor. Thousands of actors every day blow an audition because they pronounce a word wrong in the script.

As well as knowing words, again know the history of the field or the history of the project. If someone says the scene should be like a Beckett play, do you know what that means? If a film callback should have a 'Chaplinesque' feel do you know what that reference means? If the director says you remind him of Chuck Bronson and can you enhance that, do you know who that is? Do you know what text is like if they say it is, "Very like a Mamet play"? Knowing your field not only helps you in your auditions and callbacks and in doing the actual work when you get hired, but it also shows real respect for those who came before you, the creators and visionaries and writers in your field. If you want to have a future career you must learn about and respect the past within your field.

11

THE ART OF THE SELF TAPE
FOR STAGE OR FILM

I only book the gigs I am *sure* I will not get.

> David (Dave) Marantz, award winning audiobook
> narrator and actor – listen to his audiobooks if you
> want to hear a real professional

The relatively new digital self tape trend that is taking over live auditioning is the grandchild of the VHS cassette tape days of the 1970s and 1980s. Back then, a rare actor might be asked to video tape an audition and send it to a casting director. Or an already well known actor might tape a very specific audition for a very specific role (an example is the actor Elijah Wood sending in a tape to Peter Jackson for his *The Hobbit* audition). However, in 2018 the self taping has become something entirely different and is vital for actors to learn how to do well.

The Growing Art of Self Tape

Digital self taping made up maybe 10 percent or so of general national publicized auditions in 2015, then 25 percent of nearly all auditions in 2016 and over 35 percent in 2017. I predict it will grow even more in coming years. It is possible that by the year 2020 more than 75 percent of auditions will not be live, whether for stage or film. Casting directors currently may not agree with that estimate (especially those who cast solely for the stage), but in all the books about acting, casting and auditions written twenty years ago every single casting director without exception said that computerized online or non-live auditions would never, ever become a big deal in the industry. Wrong. They are now instead becoming the status quo.

It is much cheaper and much less stressful for the casting staff of a film or play to sit back and review digital audition tapes and then choose the fifteen actors they really want to meet with, as opposed to booking audition spaces in different cities, flying or driving in, seeing thousands and thousands of people in two days, spending nights in hotels away from their families and so forth. Simply receiving self tapes at their office by email or via a platform like Eco Cast is easier and cheaper. They can then view them in comfort without having to even talk to real actors. Sad, but true. So, actors must make their self tapes really count.

The Basics

A great basic of the art of self taping is, of course, to have a nice background, but do not feel you must spend hundreds of dollars on it. There will be gasps of horror in the industry as I say this, but if it looks good we do not care what you spent on your backdrop. If you are an actor, chances are that you will not have the hundreds of dollars to spend. If the audition's requested background color is a dark blue and you only have a dark blue beach towel, then thumbtack it to the wall and film in front of it. Chances are that we will never know that it is a towel, as we will not see it clearly enough to care. If you can wear something the role might wear, without being costume-y, then do so. Read the scene with someone else and look at them, not at some vague place up to the left. Eyeline is vital and we do notice if you do not have clear eye contact with your reader. Have one main point of focus and keep your eyeline there. These are some of the very basics. More to follow. First, though, is some technical information that is vital to your self-taping.

Eco Cast is an enormous online platform for audition submissions. If you have Actors Access as an online casting site, you will then get both Showfax and Eco Cast as part of your $68 per year subscription. You will then submit for an audition and if chosen you will get emailed an invite to submit an audition self tape, both in your Actors Access and also in your Eco Cast account. You then self tape it, attach it and upload it to them. Eco Cast takes it from there and sends it on to the casting office; if you submit to Eco Cast by their deadline you can be assured your self tape will be seen by the casting director. Actors who are not familiar with Eco Cast need to become so. Learn about the technology in your industry.

The Technical Stuff

The types of formats for video and audio files you send can vary, but I always advise my students to have their acting reels (which you can also send in with your initial submission) in at least two different formats, perhaps in .mp4 and .mov (and again, if you do not know what those terms mean, get very computer savvy very soon – take a basic computer class). This goes for audio reels as well, although they might be in both .mp3 and .wav formats. Having a file converter program installed on your computer is also a good thing, so that you can convert any reel immediately to the needed format and send it out. In order to deal with the technical requirements of auditions and issues with digital files and have more control over your own career, all actors need to become much more technically inclined. The internet can teach you many things – make use of it. Learn how to edit film, convert files, film your own clips and work with your own headshots and audio files.

Exercises to Practise Self Taping

Using the guidelines below, film three or so self tapes of a scene or monologue and be brutally honest (or invite three actor friends to be brutally honest) about what you see on the film. Is it clear, both in terms of the visual and audio tracks? Are you framed well? Are your eyes focused where they should be? If you are reading a scene with a parent, is your eyeline taller than you? If you are reading with a child, is your eyeline lower? If you are reading into the camera, are you really looking into the camera and connecting, or at an area around it? Or do we see zombie eyes with no connection at all? If you are not reading to the camera, are you at a three-quarter profile off to either the left or right? Is your background all one color, with no door knobs or cats or plants or anything distracting in it? Can your reader be heard and are they reading at the right volume? Not too loud, but not too soft is what you want from them. You must practise all of this so that you will be in control of the scene.

In a recent 2018 article in *Backstage*, Joseph Pearlman, a fairly well known acting coach, says that he tells his celebrity clients not to slate when they submit self tapes so they may stand out and so you, dear reader, should not slate either in order to make yourself stand out. I disagree. If you are not a celebrity, then you need to slate unless they ask you not to. In my opinion even celebrities should slate as not slating says to a casting person, "I am very well known and snooty and cannot be bothered to slate to you." You can stand out by acting well, not by showing off a large ego by forgetting to slate deliberately. The only time ever that you do not slate is when the casting people say, "Do not slate."

Self Taping – The Real Practical Do and Do Not List

1. Check the sound level on your audition before you send it off. Many actors are hyper concerned with their physical appearance, but make sure you look good *and* sound good as well. If they cannot hear your name or half of your lines, they will delete your audition before they even can see you act.

2. Unless they specifically request that you have another actor on film with you, never put another actor into your audition on camera. *Ever*. The audition is about you, not anyone else. If you cannot get another actor to do this on short notice can you do scenes with yourself? I get asked about this often. Yes. You can record the other part of the scene leaving pauses and then play that and record and do a scene with your voice as the other role. I have done this twice with tight deadlines on auditions and have booked the roles after doing it, so in a pinch it does just fine. If you do ask another actor to read with you, be sure they can be heard, but are not so great that we then want to cast them and not you. I know a young actor whose mother had the idea to put the cute boy next door live into her audition scene with her and, yes, they did get a callback from Nickelodeon, but not for her, for the neighbor boy!

3. You control the time on tape, unlike a live audition where you are nervous and rushed, so take the time to think, pause, act and

reveal yourself to us as an actor. Do not be afraid of silences. Do multiple takes of the scene (usually your third or fourth take is the best anyway) and play with pauses. Casting directors do not get to see many actors who are comfortable with pauses and silences. Let yourself think on film and take a moment.

4. Be an actor who is comfortable using silence and transitions. Everyone talks a lot and talks very fast in most self tapes. You be the one who uses transitions and silence. They want to see this. They want confidence even in your slate.

5. Self tape only inside. *Do not* film outside where you cannot control the environment, lighting, bugs, cars, helicopters, wind. Always film indoors unless they request the opposite. A college friend of mine, back in the days when you sent in an actual physical tape, sent in a self tape and got it sent back from a studio audition with a request that he never send anything to them again. When he asked us to watch it and see what he did wrong (because he just could not see it in watching himself on the tape), we noticed he was fine, but that a block behind him there were two dogs 'humping' like mad, as he had filmed it outside to be cool. It was so very not cool, although it was very funny and sort of gross. The dogs completely negated the fact that he was a really brilliant actor. You cannot control any video aspects outside. Film inside.

6. Make certain your digital self tape is in the correct format. Do they want a .mov file? .mp4? Check and always get it converted if you have to. If you send it in the wrong format they will not watch it and they certainly will not convert it for you.

7. Unless they instruct you to act directly to the camera, or to direct your scene responses into the camera, only speak to the camera for the slate. Otherwise address slightly left or right of camera. If you are framed at the shoulders then keep your movements tiny; camera choreography is essential. Hold your text up and to the side as well, or be completely memorized, so we do not see your head bobbing up and down to look at lines that you hold low at chest level. Why actors hold lines or scripts down at their chest amazes me – simply raise your hand up to be level with your eyeline, but to the left or right. You can see the text, your face is in the frame fully and we get no head bobbing on film.

8. Remember to slate in the self tape. Do not get so focused on technical details that you forget this and always view your entire self tape before you send it out. If you edit it all yourself, so much the better.

9. So, how to end the tape rather than an abrupt cut to black. Either cut to darkness after a large beat after your last line, or turn to camera after a beat when scene is done and say 'thank you'. Both work just fine and they end it well, as does a classy and classic fade to black. Do not end it with us seeing you reach out and fumble to turn off the camera.

10. Stick to the stated deadlines. Eco Cast may be the hosting platform you send your tape to or you may send it directly to a casting office. Either way, if the deadline is Friday at midnight, you should send it in twelve to twenty-four hours before that at the latest. Audition tapes and emails stack up to be processed and the stack of tapes left in the email line at deadline are often tossed. Get yours in early so it is sure to be seen. When an actor says to me, "I got it sent in with ten minutes to spare", I just shake my head. Chances are very good it will never be seen.

11. If you can, let them see your full body at some point in your tape. Many people show their full body before the slate and then slowly zoom in to go to close up. They just want to see your body type or look. If they are matching you to be the daughter of Frances McDormand then they need to get a glimpse of your physical type.

This is also a vital step in self tape auditions for children, who are often cast not because they are the best actor, but because they are the best match for the role's physical type, height, hair color or body shape. Parents, be sure to include a full body shot of your child in any taped auditions where you know your child is auditioning for a member of a family. I hate to say it, but often the questions are, "Is the kid cute? And do they look like so-and-so?" Very often the question is not whether the kid is the best actor for the role.

Give yourself every possible advantage when you self tape. Practise, review, pay attention to detail. Get it done and in early; memorize it if you can. Put the same effort into a self tape that you do for a live audition. In fact, put more effort into it, as you have no 'live' meet to make them love you. They must love you from that self tape.

12

ON THE SET:
WHAT YOU NEED TO KNOW

Being an actor on a movie set is like going to the playground at recess.

Melissa Leo

Before you place a foot on a set for any filmed media you will receive, usually by email now, a call sheet. It is the equivalent of a rehearsal schedule for the theater, plus a layout of the entire day on the set to come. You will get it at least twenty-four hours ahead of time. Rather than put one in this book I invite you to search for it online and you can view many examples.

The Call Sheet

This call sheet not only lets you know your timeline for the next day (when are you picked up at the hotel, when are you in hair and makeup, when are you scheduled to be on the set), but it also lets you know precisely which scenes you and other actors are filming that day. Most of the time you will not film scenes in sequence; you will film around the availability of locations or the lead actors and their availability. Perhaps you have the office set only for tomorrow so only the scenes filmed on that set will be shot then. Your call sheet lets you know whatever scenes you are in the next day, so you will need to be prepared that next day and ready to go with those scenes whether they are in sequence for your character or not.

Do not be married to what you may do in the film or television scene. Do not pre-emptively decide about the tone, breathing, acting choices or the line delivery. 'Pink sheets' are legendary in that medium. Pink sheets are sometimes handed to you the morning of a shoot, sometimes very shortly before a shoot, and they are all the rewrites of the scene and your lines. You are expected to memorize them on the fly. This does not happen all the time, but it does happen, and the sheets do not have to be pink, but you will encounter them at one point or another on a set. I once worked on a set where there were pink sheets, yellow sheets (rewrites of the pink sheets) and blue sheets (the newest cuts and additions to the yellow sheets) with the end results being making our scripts look like rainbows. These were not very happy rainbows in that there was much rememorizing. Not all rewrites are bad – in fact most are good – but always be ready to stuff new lines into your head if you need to.

Tips for the First Day on Set

The first time you ever step on a film or TV set it is an amazing, frightening, intimidating and wonderful thing all at once. There is a lot to keep straight, so here are some good tips. During your first time on a set you may also think that 'action' is the word you are listening for in order to act. I do not agree. 'Action' is when the film is already rolling, not when you begin to prepare. So, you should listen for 'speed', which is the word usually said before 'action'. Then the moment 'action!' is said you are already focused, not getting ready to think about how to focus. Once action is said, if you have the line that starts the scene, take a second (or longer if you have been directed to pause) and then just say it. You will be focused. Simple.

Understand that, unless you are the star of the project, you are very low in the hierarchy. Usually you will meet anywhere from three to five assistant directors, or ADs, right off the bat – why are there so many? Because one deals primarily with technical things, another with logistics of crew and catering, and one mainly deals with actors (and this is the one that you should be sure that you remember). Once you do meet them, check in with that AD and then you will be rushed into hair, makeup and costume (where you will be gracious and have your size sheet ready and be nice to everyone). Then, you will wait. Then you will usually sit and wait some more. Then you will hear, "Actors, please for line up!"

The Line Up

A line up is not filming the scene. A line up is very similar to setting blocking in a theatrical production and often the line up may be the very first time you actually meet the other actors in the scene with you. If you do TV work you will get some rehearsal time, usually, on the set or in a separate rehearsal room. But on a film set this line up may be the only rehearsal opportunity you ever get with the other actors. Each actor is walked through all the positions of their blocking in the scene and at each move a production assistant will mark an X on the floor, in fluorescent tape, where you stand. Keep track of the color of the tape in that scene as each actor has a different color and it can change from scene to scene and day to day. Your first place is your "one", your second place is your "two" and so forth. You all then go to your one, your two and so forth, and you are then blocked. Sometimes you do not rehearse the scene at all, but just simply get your blocking. Then you shoot the scene, right? Nope. Then you go sit and relax and wait some more. Oh, and then you wait some more.

On a film set you will soon adjust to being open to the many ways the scene can go; you will adjust for stamina needed for repeated takes and you will also learn to save energy for your close ups or your very high emotional moments. As opposed to the stage, where you must be 'on point' every second for two hours for the audience, with the show then over until the next night, on a film set you will work very intensely on a scene, perhaps for an entire day, and then probably never work on it again. It is a shorter period of focus, but it is very intense.

Microphones and their Perils

For work on a set you will encounter a few different types of microphones. Everyone knows what a boom mic is, the long fuzzily covered microphone held on the end of a pole. It is held above a scene and catches the general sound from everyone as it 'booms' out (this is a great way to remember what it is called). There are also body microphones and many actors will not encounter these until on a set. A body mic is a tiny microphone on the end of a long wire and attached to a battery pack, about the size of a cell phone, which weighs a few pounds. The battery is usually placed in the small of an actor's back and strapped in with an elastic band or tape. Then the wire is threaded up under the shirt and hidden somewhere in the neckline of the clothing. These and body mics like these are also used on Broadway now, as well as stage microphones put around the set and hung overhead.

There are three rules of body mics that you should never forget. First, always assume they are 'live' and recording, even if you are certain it has been turned off. Do not yack off set with someone about how dumb the director is or how you hate being in this film. Assume your microphone is recording at all times. Actors get fired for mouthing off when they think their mic is off. Second, never thump your chest or clutch anything in the area of that tiny microphone hidden in your collar. It does no good to be acting brilliantly if you have just crushed the microphone in your hand and ruined the sound. The third rule applies much more to those who identify as females than males as they tend to sit more in the restroom. As the battery pack is situated in your lower back area right above your buttocks, always find a sound person and ask for the battery pack to be removed before you go to the restroom. They will remove it and then usually wait right outside the restroom and hook it right back up when you are done. This is for two reasons, one of which is obvious. You do not want a microphone recording your live bathroom performance in any way (I have heard 'live' bathroom performance clips played at the wrap party more than a few times and have always been grateful I was not the one who was taped). The other reason is that if you forget that the battery is on your lower back and go to sit down, whipping your pants past your butt, that battery goes right into the toilet. You do not want to be the infamous and horrified actor who carries a dripping wet $2,000 battery pack to the sound person for replacement.

Speaking of butts (a lame segue to be sure!), another thing to know is how to cover your butt on the set. When the director is done shooting your scenes for the day and you are told you are 'wrapped', say thanks but do not run off back to the hotel just yet. Find the AD who deals with the actors and double check with him or her that you are indeed wrapped, or done for the day. Once the AD says you are wrapped, then you can finally take off. Why double check with the

AD? Because if the director changes his mind five minutes after he tells you that you are wrapped and then he decides that he wants you back on the set, you do not want it to be your fault that you left. Because you first double checked with the AD, it is now their fault that you left. The AD knows this and knows it is part of their job to bear the brunt of this, but you want your own reputation to be spotless.

The Scene Takes How Long?

Now let's say on your first day on the set, you are in one scene with two other actors and it is only three pages long. Easy, right? Should only take a few hours to film, right? Nope. Let me walk you through why often that scene may take eight hours to film or longer. If your scene involves any extra physicality, such as kissing, sex, fights, punches, dancing, singing, stunts, blue or green screen work, CGI, motion capture and more, you can be assured the scene could take up to a week or more to film.

A three page scene with three actors will be blocked during a line up and then you will wait until cameras and lights are set and focused and are ready, and then you will come to the set and shoot. Usually you will shoot your master shot first. This 'master' is a shot that covers all the actors, the entire room, all the blocking moves and the entire scene in one continuous take. It gets 'coverage' of everything and everyone in the scene. Coverage is a word you will hear a lot on film sets. Coverage means footage of film of every actor from every possible angle in order to have more options during the editing process. They may even check your coverage throughout the day, "Do we have enough coverage on her?", they'll ask the director or cinematographer before wrapping you for the day.

Your master shot may have anywhere from one to fifteen or more takes. An important thing to remember is that you, unless you are directed to, do not want to make any large physical movements in the master shot because if you do then you will have to match them, the exact same movement on the same exact word, in every other shot that includes that line or word. Most of the time actors stick to the blocking in the master shot as they do not want to have to remember what word they moved their hand on for the rest of every shot within the scene. A master shot that does maybe five takes will take at least an hour or two to shoot for them to talk and refocus and direct you between takes. Then you take a break for at least half an hour while they refocus lights and camera for the next angle of the scene. Then you move on sometimes to 'twofers' where the same scene is shot again, yet the camera is only focused on two people in the scene for four or five or so takes, for another hour. Then a 'twofer' shot of the other half of the scene for another hour or more. Then a break for repositioning of camera and lights. Then maybe close ups of actor one and all their lines for an hour, then close ups of actor two for an hour, then close ups of you for an hour. That is already seven working hours, not including lunch, and they have not even shot any point of view (POV) shots over someone's shoulder, or close up specialty shots of your hands as you talk or the curtain blowing in the breeze. This is how a short scene can take a day or two. This can get even more complicated with an exterior (EXT) scene shot outdoors, as opposed to an interior (INT) scene.

Stamina and Repetition on the Set and at Home

How can you prepare for this on set stamina and repetition at home? That is difficult, but you can prepare your stamina for repetition of scenes, monologues and moments in those scenes by practising them in every possible way. Take a line and give it ten different real readings. Take an audition monologue and treat it as a comedy piece, then a drama, then do it as a psychopath, then as a cheerleader. Learn physical and breath stamina and to be very flexible with text. The more you can approach text with no preconceived notions or decisions and patterns the more you will book roles and move into filming them much more seamlessly.

The Size Sheet

There is yet another way you can walk into a role simply by ensuring you are in the right place at the right time. A sheet of measurements, a 'size sheet', is something I tell my students to keep current and always have a hard copy of. Have all your measurements done (and even the odd ones, glove size and hat size) and keep that sheet

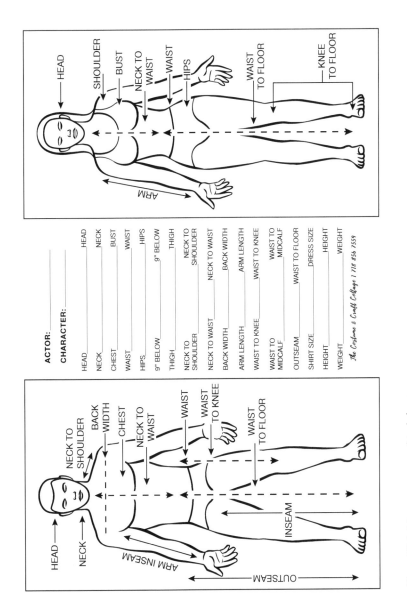

ACTOR: _____

CHARACTER: _____

HEAD _____	HEAD
NECK _____	NECK
CHEST _____	BUST
WAIST _____	WAIST
HIPS _____	HIPS
9" BELOW _____	9" BELOW
THIGH _____	THIGH
NECK TO SHOULDER _____	NECK TO SHOULDER
NECK TO WAIST _____	NECK TO WAIST
BACK WIDTH _____	BACK WIDTH
ARM LENGTH _____	ARM LENGTH
WAIST TO KNEE _____	WAIST TO KNEE
WAIST TO MIDCALF _____	WAIST TO MIDCALF
OUTSEAM _____	WAIST TO FLOOR
SHIRT SIZE _____	DRESS SIZE
HEIGHT _____	HEIGHT
WEIGHT _____	WEIGHT

The Costume & Craft College 1 118 856 1559

Figure 12.1 Measurement, or 'size' sheet

both digitally and in hard copy. Why? Because if you and six other actors are all playing students of Leo DiCaprio in his next film and all six of you actors show up on the set at the same time, the first place you will go is to get into costumes. Inevitably the head costumer will enquire if anyone knows their sizes. This is when you say, "I do!", and hand her all your measurements. She will love you for it and then you will most likely be the first of the six of you in costume. Then while the other five actors are being measured by her staff for the next forty-five minutes you will be in and out of makeup and the first one on the set. Just in time to meet the director, the assistant director, and to share a bagel with Leo.

Does this guarantee you fame? No. (Although, I went to college with an actor who got his big break by being first one on the set simply by doing the above. An actor had to be replaced and there he was, the first one on the set having coffee, and got an improvised audition on the set, which he aced. Big break done!) What it does guarantee you is some good networking time and the time to make a solo impression on other actors and the staff and crew. Then later in the day, when they do shoot a 'wild scene' or 'wild lines' (a scene or lines that is not in the written final shooting script), most likely they will say, "Hey, let that kid who ate the bagel with Leo be in the wild scene. Let's put that kid in the elevator with Leo." Then you suddenly go from 'one of the six students' to 'that guy in the elevator scene with Leo Dicaprio'. See the difference? Sometimes that wild line or wild scene can even get you a signed contract or a union card right there on the spot.

Framing

An important thing to remember on the set, unlike on stage, is that the only reality is in 'the frame'. The frame is the box you are in while being filmed and where you are framed is important (framing you at the neck means there can really be no movement above the neck as your head fills the screen, framing at the waist means you can use your arms and do not have to be as confined within the frame). You should always have a good idea of where you are being framed in any shot and I teach my students to ask the camera operator this in film auditions right before they slate as well. You audition much better if you know how wide or tight you are being shot. You play better if you know the size of your playground.

I have been on a set and have watched a very well known actor preparing for a dramatic close up. The actor was simultaneously chewing gum and smoking a cigarette while his makeup and hair were adjusted. He then asked, "Where are you framing me again?", and was told, "At your shoulders". He nodded. When the moment before action was called, he blew his last puff of smoke out of his mouth, palmed his gum, and held his gum and lit cigarette in one hand out of frame at about waist level. He then acted a gorgeous and relaxed take of his lines and, as soon as "cut" was called, he popped the gum right back into his mouth and took a deep drag of his cigarette. Again, the only thing that mattered in that shot was what was in the frame. Listen on the set, know what the shot is about and where the frame is. Pay attention at all times even if you are not in the shot.

How can you practise framing on your own? It helps to think of what framing really is in a movie. Yes, it is how the camera sees you inside that 'little box'. However it is so much more than that. It is how the cinematographer sees the entire scene as a picture. It is how a director sees an entire storyboard of the film. It is how the audience understands the image, moment, emotion, scene or the whole story. Framing images is how the entire film is communicated visually, frame by frame. The next time you watch a movie, watch it with the framing in your mind. You will see it and appreciate it in a whole new way. You will realize how much framed images mean to you in your own viewer history of film watching. You will become frame conscious. Then you can begin to do exercises at home to practise it.

Camera choreography is an issue that comes up in auditions a great deal. Think of camera choreography and framing just like the use of stage blocking. On stage usually an actor is directed to move and then to talk after he moves so as not to lose what lines the actor says because he is moving across a long stage. With more naturalistic theater, of course, actors move and talk at the same time. For movement on camera I do recommend that actors move then talk, especially when newer to working in closeup shots. The tighter the shot, the less you can move; even your eyes and facial muscles must be calmer the closer the camera is to you (unless it is a deliberate choice by you and the director to have some odd, kinetic movement in a close up shot).

The slower the movement, the easier it is to watch in a movie theater when your head is the size of an SUV on the screen. The slower the movement, the easier it is for the camera to follow you as you move or for the audience to see what you are feeling. Good actors learn how to control their movement according to the frame or the camera movement need. Wider frames can support wider or larger movements. Tighter frames demand less movement. Head tilts, head bobs, or shifting from foot to foot are all bad habits of which you should rid yourself. These are habits you can work on losing when you are on camera or in any audition. They distract us from really seeing you and will cost you work.

Exercise for Framing and Camera Choreography

Do exercises by frame in order to practise your movement. Film your audition monologue many times: once in an ECU (which means extreme close up – framing you from your chin to the top of your head), then in CU (close up – from your Adam's apple to a few inches over your head), then at your shoulders, then at your chest, then at your waist and then at full body. Six times. Do the monologue exactly the same each time and study what movements are too much for each frame size and which are just right and which are out of the frame entirely. Then do the same exercise all over again, but change and adjust each sequence of movements for the frame size. If you can go from a full body, physically expressive monologue that is within the frame and is frame appropriate to an extreme close up where you barely move your face and eyes, then you will begin to understand camera choreography and how it applies to different frames.

Exercises to help with framing are workable in two ways. Ask everyone you know to film you, even just short clips on their iPhones, and then look at the results so that you begin to understand yourself within the frame, and to understand how much you can move or not move depending upon where you are framed. Also, an exercise that I love is to begin to actively notice mirrors and reflective surfaces wherever you go and see where you are framed in them. Are you riding a bus or subway? Look in the window, how does it frame you? How do shop windows frame you? Learn to see the world around you and yourself by how and when you are framed in various things.

Begin to look at it as a director or cinematographer does and you will also be consciously practising framing.

In film and TV work you may often end up having no rehearsals at all. You must walk onto a set understanding what you want to do with a role and knowing who you are playing. Notice I did not say 'how' you are playing. The worst thing you can do in theater or film is to pre-decide how you will say something. Do not memorize with breaths, pauses and intonation set in stone or you will have a very difficult time on set when you may need fifteen takes (and fifteen totally different ways of saying that line) to get the scene shot. You may only meet the other actors when you arrive on set and you will have no idea what their talents are or how the scene will go, so be very open to playing on the set. Your project may film in ten days or three months, but it is a considerably shorter time than theater takes and you will wait around on set a *lot*. So, is any stamina required? Yes, when you are on take twenty-six of your screaming argument – you will realize stamina is needed.

However, it is a shorter term stamina, needed for an eight or ten hour day on the set and then usually never again for that scene (as opposed to a stage role where you only need stamina for two hours a night on the stage, but your show may run for six months or even longer). This shorter term on set stamina must be real on every level as the camera is not fifteen rows away like in the theater. Usually the camera will be right up in your face, at least for some of the shots. In film you can think and the camera sees it. You do not need to 'act'.

Intimate Scenes

Actors also deal with intimate scenes and sexuality and sometimes inappropriate behavior (both on stage and on film). You should never be asked to do anything intimate (kiss, disrobe, fondle, etc.) with anyone, ever, in any audition. You may be asked to in a callback, but that is still rare and if it does happen you would be told in detail before arriving at the callback. You should never be asked to disrobe until the day of the shoot of 'that' scene or on a pre-decided day in a play rehearsal. You can be cast without you needing to make out with anyone or be naked. If you stand in front of me at an audition I can easily see whether you have body parts or not. I do not need to see them naked. Producers, directors or casting directors may not – under any circumstances – require actors to disrobe in an audition, as per SAG-AFTRA rules. It does not matter if you are union or not, if the production is a SAG-AFTRA signatory production, they cannot do this. If this happens to you it is not only your right, but your job to report them. The reality is that, even if it is not a union job, you should report them. No job *ever* is worth it. The non reporting only encourages the continuation of the abuse with other actors and actresses. I have been semi nude on film and completely naked in three different stage shows, so I know of what I speak!

How then do these 'skin scenes' work in real life on set or on stage? How should intimate scenes be handled? They should be fully talked through in a comfortable and fully clothed setting first, literally step by step and in a technical fashion, by the actors and director. There is nothing left to chance, misinterpretation or 'improvising'. Period. Not a kiss, not a touch, not the movement of one finger. It is all completely choreographed. In film or stage productions I work on I treat intimate scenes as importantly as I treat the combat scenes. They are discussed by all in them and choreographed to the smallest detail and are blocked out very early in the rehearsal or shooting process. You should also always have, or you should demand, a locked set, a locked rehearsal, and only very limited staff or crew when filming or rehearsing with any skin showing. Robes are usually provided for all actors on the day of filming or disrobing (you do not want to sit around naked while getting notes) and if you know robes are not provided then bring your own. There are no pictures taken (although production art shots may be decided on later, again by everyone, for PR or publicity needs). You can even request an on set monitor of the intimacy and behavior within the scene. If you are in a stage or film production that is not adhering to these very simple rules, you can contact Intimacy Directors International or your agent, if you have one. You can also contact unions if there are any issues at all. You can contact other actors, directors, heck even contact me. However, speak up if you must because not doing so helps those perpetrators continue to be inappropriate. You, and other artists, deserve better.

The Screen Actors Guild released an initiative in February 2018 called 'The Four Pillars of Change: Confronting Harassment and

Advancing Equity'. They will develop materials that give members a clear understanding of their rights in the workplace and provide reliable guidance to navigate the unique environments of the entertainment and media industries. They will:

- disseminate and clarify protections for employees, including those that flow from the law, our collective bargaining agreements, applicable policies and other regulations;
- establish a Code of Conduct along with scenario-specific guidance that outlines best practices and offers practical insights for members on how to avoid and/or address sexual harassment in the workplace and related environments;
- communicate clear expectations that members will refrain from harassing conduct;
- provide guidance for members who experience or witness sexual harassment;
- provide information for reporting sexual harassment and the resources to support members seeking assistance;
- these materials will be developed in consultation with our members and with guidance from subject matter experts.

Actors' Equity and the theater community have risen to this occasion as well. Theaters in 2016 in Chicago (Director Darrell Cox was the focus of abuse allegations at Profiles Theater) began their Chicago Theater Standards and the #notinourhouse campaign, and other places such as The Alley Theatre in Houston, Texas, faced scandals due to inappropriate physicality both on and off stage. With the subsequent 2017 scandal regarding high powered Hollywood producer Harvey Weinstein (among many others), I think it is even more vital for this understanding about what is right to be a substantially integrated part of the theatrical, dance, film audition and production processes. The moment you feel that you are being pushed, touched or made to feel physically, emotionally or sexually uncomfortable you need to speak up. Right then and there. Male or female, gay or straight, young or old, black or white or brown, nobody has the right to make you feel sexually harassed – even if they are a big Oscar winner or even your favorite actor ever. Being treated badly is not the price you must pay for getting cast. It is wrong, period.

On January 16, 2018 the strongest initiative towards education
and mediation when it comes to sexual harassment within the theater
industry was put in motion. Actress Marin Ireland and Attorney
Norman Siegel, with the support of all of the theatrical unions and
guilds, launched the Theatrical Community Sexual Harassment
Education and Mediation Pilot Project (Pilot Project for short).

> Under the education component, the Pilot Project will set out to
> provide written material informing individuals of their rights
> regarding sexual harassment, sexual discrimination, sexual abuse,
> and criminal conduct. Through an affiliation with New York
> theaters, the project encourages artistic directors to make a state-
> ment at every show's first company meeting clearly explaining
> what constitutes sexual harassment and the theater's zero-tolerance
> policy. Every person working on the production will be given the
> names of the theater's Human Resources department, Actor's
> Equity (who has worked with the Pilot Project to train business
> reps to address sexual harassment complaints), as well as the correct
> point of contact at the Actor's Fund – should such an incident
> occur. The cast and crew, as well as the staff at the theater, will
> also be given information on how to participate in the Pilot
> Project's mediation process.
>
> The mediation sector will give individuals in the theater
> industry who are involved in incidents of non-criminal sexual
> harassment the option of engaging in a confidential mediation pro-
> cess overseen by a neutral certified mediator (volunteers will be
> working pro bono during the six-month test period). Possible
> resolutions as a result of mediation could include: an apology, a
> commitment to end unwanted behavior of a sexual nature – and
> in some instances, future counseling.

These initiatives, then, at least in the theater and film world, are a
start. There is more about this and a link to the websites in the
resources section.

13

ON THE STAGE:
WHAT YOU NEED TO KNOW

Who'da thunk I could sing, right? But it's a great tour and once it's done, something else that's great will happen.

Pre-*Law & Order* Jerry Orbach, backstage while on tour in *Chicago*

We will not address the basics of a stage and how to move on it – let us be honest, if you do not know stage basics like upstage and stage right, you need to learn them. This book is not the place to do so, but, if you are planning on walking into an audition not knowing what to do when asked to move 'down left', then you will have already probably blown the audition. An audition is never the place to learn or be taught the basics, unless you have a very kind casting director who has that as part of the casting process with new actors. Know the layout of a stage, know stage directions, know how to notate them fast in your script with the correct abbreviations (XDR means cross down right, for instance, as opposed to having to write 'I then cross down stage right . . .' while other actors stand and wait for you to finish), know how to enunciate, know how to project your voice.

Even in a film audition you still may be asked to move downstage left so you really need to know what that means. If you look at a casting person blankly when they say this, they really will not cast you. Not because they think that you have no talent, but because they usually just do not have time to teach you the basics on the stage or in a film if they cast you in the role.

If you are very lucky you may get to work on a brand new play, in a new role that nobody has ever performed before, and you may have the playwright around during your rehearsal and development process to edit, tighten, adjust and rewrite the text. They may indeed change text and scenes specifically because of something you said or did in rehearsal or even when you were goofing around. This is a great gift, as often you can gain many insights into your role that normally actors never get to inquire of the playwright. Take advantage of this when you can and memorize any alterations immediately. Usually your director will set a date by which there are to be no more script rewrites or changes, but that is not always the case. There are always the stories of lines being changed two days before opening night. Be well prepared and know what you are doing and who the role is, and you will weather all this happening.

So, the difference in stage and film acting stamina is, and this is reiterated a few times in this book, that stage acting requires anywhere from three to twelve or more weeks of rehearsals (and in a union contract you may rehearse eight hours a day, five days a week, or shorter hours for six days a week). You then look forward to performing the show for anywhere from three weeks to years (if you are on tour or on Broadway, for instance, you may do a show for ten years or more). The stamina is very long term, but can be less 'real' at times depending on the role or how far away the audience is. If you know you are in the back row for thirty minutes, and you do eight shows a week on tour, you can conserve energy but still be present and acting during that thirty minutes you are not the focus of the play. I know stage actors who have unfortunately been on complete autopilot on stage and the audience may not even be able to tell. I have seen actors on Broadway in leading roles on full autopilot and the audience *can* tell. This does not mean it is right if they do it or that it is right if you are the focus of the scene, however. Film demands less long term stamina as, once a scene is shot, you are done with it, but you may film that scene twenty-four or even fifty times in a ten hour day, or you may film that scene from every angle for two weeks.

Understudying

Understudying roles is only for stage roles. I do get asked a lot, "Should I do it?" I have heard many actors say they would never understudy a role. Usually these are newer, younger actors who actually need the stage time and work experience that understudying would give them. My vote is that you should always take an understudy role (especially any regional, off-Broadway or Broadway or any union and paying work), as that is a great place to learn, to watch the professionals, and to network. I have understudied three times in my career and two of those times I ended up playing the role for the entire run of the show. Always take the understudy role is my advice, as you gain experience, network with others and continue to grow as an artist. If it is a paying gig, generally the golden rule is to take the role at all times. Needing to pay your bills is pretty important.

As well, all the times I and others have understudied we have inevitably been cast in other shows in better and bigger roles by the very directors we understudied for initially. I myself have had actors understudy in a show I directed, whom I then loved as understudies and cast them in future shows in the leading role.

Another thing that will endear you to a director is coming to them when you have a problem that may affect the show, *but* with a viable solution to that problem in hand. Case in point – in 2015 I was directing *Richard III* in New York City and a lovely actor named Perri Yaniv was playing Clarence. Perri is a very talented and busy actor and ended up having a conflict with the performances and another show he wanted to do. However, by the time he approached me he laid out the problem *and* the solution in the form of his dear friend Jessica Leventhal. Jessica was an equally wonderful actor and their joint proposal was that they both rehearse the role in *Richard III* and then split the performances, thus letting him do both shows, letting me have the role filled with two wonderful actors and letting Jessica work with us in a great part. Of course I said yes and it was not only a smart move on Perri's part, but a very respectful and professional one. Coming to me with both a problem and a solution made it easy to say yes and to deal with, and that let me know how conscientious he was as a human being with my time and energy. Would I hire him again? In a heartbeat. I would hire Jessica too. Everyone wins.

There is one thing that is a stage issue much more so than a film issue, and that will kill not only an audition, but can damage the rehearsal process as well. That is when actors make the mistake of playing the end of the play or film. With newly written films you rarely know the full script, but with plays you can usually read them if they are already published. So in order to not kill an initial audition, if you do know the end of the script (you are the killer everyone is searching for! Or, you die of leukemia and it is horrible!), do not even play a hint of it unless you are directed to. I once gave auditionees a scene and told them it was from the beginning of the play, but that she died at the end of the play. She actually did not die at the end, but I wanted to see what would happen at the audition. Probably 65 percent of the actresses auditioning suddenly developed coughs and sighs and very pained looks. The ones who did not develop these things got seriously considered and then called back. If you know the end of the play and you do die of leukemia, play the opposite in the early scenes. Play as if you are the healthiest and happiest person ever. Plays and scenes have an arc for a reason. How are you different at the beginning and end of the play? If you die at the end, you need an arc to get there, so work on playing the opposite of that and give yourself a place to start.

Memorizing Your Lines

I have also come to believe over the years as both an actor and director that there are very differing levels of memorization for both stage and film. Stage trained actors are infinitely better memorizers than film actors with no stage training, as the new trend in film acting is not memorizing at all in order to make it more 'real'. This is not acting: it is making up lines and self indulgence. Actors memorize lines and do it well; they work on lines and then make it *seem* effortless. That is precisely what acting is. "Actors" who want to be in film who do not memorize lines are not acting like professional actors. Period. They may get paid, but they are not true professionals in my book. This is not to be confused with improvisation – I am speaking of a role with lines where an actor who does not do his or her job and memorize them.

Even 'professionals' may be very unprofessional, as in the 2015–2016 Broadway season where both Bruce Willis and Al Pacino appeared in shows where they were leads and were fed their lines via earpieces. Mr. Pacino was in a role that had many lines and professionally he should not have taken it on if unable to memorize it. Mr. Willis was a different story, and simply was used to being able to ad lib on film without having to be stringent about memorization. In both cases the audience was negatively impacted, as were the other actors in both productions, which were panned by the critics. Memorize your lines or do not take the role. Memorize your lines or do not take on acting as a profession.

Stage actors memorizing can range from "I think I know it" all the way to "It is in the DNA" stage acting. If it is in your DNA, if someone drops a line on stage, you can jump ahead one paragraph and include their jumped line in your line, then cut back to your own original line, all without missing a beat. This is when you also are so at one with the lines that they seem to not be memorized at all and can come out differently each performance; however, the only way to make it seem effortless is to actually memorize the lines. Do the work. Whenever I have had any role, but especially a lead role with many lines, I still arrive at the theater early and sit and run my lines every single night of the performance. Every night without fail. Bill Nighy, a wonderful British actor who has made a few Broadway appearances, tends to walk to the theater and run his lines as he walks before every single show. This is what professionals do. They do not count on making it up.

When you put this much diligence into the memorizing and constant refreshing of lines, this is when they appear to be 'effortless' on stage. Actors who do not care enough to memorize well or who do not care that they continually stress the cast and director out by always being the last one to learn lines (sometimes finally getting off book a few days before the show actually opens) should know this: directors and casting people tell each other about you and warn others against casting you. Shape up.

New Stage Technology

In 2018 you may think there is nothing new to deal with as an actor in regard to stage acting. You rehearse, you do the show. Same as fifty years ago. Nope. Now you are much more appealing and marketable as an actor if you can also work with multimedia, rotating stages, stage combat, aerial rigs, trap doors, wire-work (also used in film), microphones (both handheld and body mics), puppetry (and again be specific about hand puppets, marionettes or full size body puppets) and any and all stage technology. Stunts? Pyrotechnics? Listing these on your resume (or at least understanding what they are because you have worked with them) can carry heavy weight and can help to get you future work.

The days of just showing up with lines ready are long gone. Many theaters start rehearsals with you not memorized at all and you get a long rehearsal period to learn them. Other theaters may hire you and want you at the very first rehearsal completely off book, even with no idea of the blocking in your head. But there is now far more to it than just learning the lines and blocking. Using new stage and computer techniques that have begun to merge the internet with traditional stage theater, the University of Central Florida, Bradley University in Illinois and the University of Waterloo in Canada performed a play in 2017 that put actors from Florida and Canada on the stage in Illinois without any of them ever leaving their respective campuses. Amazing. This type of collaborative theater may very well be the future of stage productions, and actors who are tech savvy and easy to work with are in high demand. I often coach scenes and auditions for actors all over the world without being in the same room or even the same country with those I am directing.

Technology is growing so fast for the stage that what I type today may be completely outdated by print time. In England a company named Knifedge and a fellow named Timothy Bird have just put a completely computer-generated avatar into a scene, sword fighting with an actor live on stage. Mr. Bird began his tech feats with a Seurat painting gradually coming to life on stage in *Sunday in the Park with George*, the show that cemented Knifedge's reputation with an Olivier award in London for Best Set Design in 2007. It is your job as an actor to keep up with news and projects like this. This is part of knowing your field in this digital age.

Projection technology has taken off for the stage as well, going far beyond the dear old scrim projections we all know and adore, with holograms now being projected and interacted with on stage in both concert and live stage performance venues. New plays are actively being written as we speak that will make use of holograms as actual characters. Older plays are even ripe for this technology as well (imagine *Macbeth* with holograms as ghosts!). Imagine what the next ten years will bring to stage technology. A smart actor will know what happens in the field and also how to work with it and talk about it.

Look Regionally at Theater

When most actors think of the stage they think of New York City. It is where Broadway is, after all. Yet, Broadway itself is made up of mostly musicals or a few 'straight plays' that always star well known actors only. And then there is also the current trend of the Hollywood Studios backing musicals as spin offs of their movie brands, not as stand alone new musicals. It is so expensive to produce musicals now that very often the only ones who can afford to produce them are the movie studios. Then they really only look for established television stars or movie actors if they can get them. This trend seems to only gain ground alongside the other current trend of filming Broadway musicals, but recasting the roles with very well known singers and celebrities for a one night viewing on television. For better or worse this trend is one I see growing even larger, as it has proven to be very lucrative.

Newer actors are wise to begin to their work on resume building in smaller local, regional, and touring markets and to look beyond New York City to the growing theater action in Los Angeles. Chicago is a great place for theater as well and continues to carry a distinction in the United States of having the highest proportion of actors working and being paid to work of any US state. Five or six years ago Albuquerque, New Mexico, was the other US hotspot for actors due to *Breaking Bad* and a few other shows being filmed there, bringing it to actors' attention. The current hotspot now is Atlanta, Georgia. In another four to six years it may be somewhere else due to a new TV show or a hot producer.

But younger actors do not always have to be in Los Angeles and New York to get experience and grow their resume. You may not be famous enough or experienced enough to play the lead in *Romeo and Juliet* in New York, but you may be perfect to do it in a lovely regional theater in Chicago, Michigan or even in Canada and to get that experience, good paycheck and the resume credit and networking. Building your resume outside the larger markets can be great if you can get the work. Build that resume well so that, when you do get to Broadway, you will be ready to wow everyone.

14

CONTRACTS: LOCAL, NATIONAL AND INTERNATIONAL

A verbal agreement is not worth the paper it is printed on.
Sir Bryan O'Loghlen, Australian/Irish politician, 1890.
This quote is often mistakenly attributed to studio
head Samuel Goldwyn

The most important thing about contracts for any artists (aside from actually reading them) is that you do not sign them and then assume that you can blow them off. You cannot ever blow off a signed contract. Once you sign any contract you commit to do the work. If that needs to change, then you need to be released from the contract and it needs to be done right and legally. Do not treat contracts lightly even if you see other actors do so, and you *will* see that. You can ruin your career by treating contracts like a joke. When you do sign them, please read them first. Seriously. Many young actors do not even read their own contracts. Do not ever get so excited about a role that you just jump and sign something that you have not read.

What to Look For in the US

What should you look for in your contracts? You need to be on the lookout for: ancillary rights (What happens with the merchandise profits for the film? What happens with the iPad application that uses your likeness for a slot machine game?); 'pay-or-play' clauses or language (if you and the director have a disagreement and he fires you from the film, you want to still get paid whether you did the actual part in the final film or not – if you have a pay or play clause you will indeed get paid); the billing order you may have; any insurance issues; your right of publicity (which has a huge impact on your career); and much more.

Can you sign contracts without being signed with an agent? Sure you can, and it happens often, but be very certain you know what to look for in those contracts so that you are truly protected. Have an attorney look at it for you as an option, but have someone help you to look at it for certain. In domestic (gigs within the fifty United States and US territories) contracts, these are some of the things you should look for: are you insured on the set; what is your billing (and often you can take less money for the role in order to have a higher billing or a separate 'card' saying 'and introducing Bob Smith as Bob') and whether you can negotiate money for better billing; a pay-or-play clause as mentioned above; transportation to and from any location you shoot the film at (and on the ground on location how do you get from your hotel to the set itself? You do not want to be having to rent a car at the last minute because that was not settled in your contract); what rooms or trailers will you be waiting in on the set between set ups and takes if you are in a remote location; what is your per diem (this means per day fee so you can eat when you are not eating the catered food on the set) and any costuming fees, particularly on indie film sets when you may be paid to use your own clothing. There can be additional information about any stunts (and to what level of difficulty you agree to do them or not do them), fight scenes, makeup, prosthetic usage (fake teeth, wigs, body parts, etc.), any intimate scenes, screen testing for all of that and so much more. Every time I hear about an actor with contract issues it usually (96 percent of the time) is a direct result of them not reading the contract in the first place before they signed it.

International Contracts

In international contracts (where you are working anywhere outside of the fifty United States and Canada) you should be looking for all of the above plus who (by name) on their production staff is setting up you with travel visas, who is setting up your shots and immunizations, and who is setting up getting you any pills (say, for malaria prevention at your shooting location or country) and any other medicines you will take with you while on location. You should not ever be doing these complicated things yourself. Are there any provisions for there to be bodyguards in the more dangerous areas of the world? If you are on set and shooting in a very remote location, how close are the medical staff, or are they on the set itself? Are there plans and contingencies set in motion for full staff and actor evacuations due to medical issues or even civil unrest? Are there daily or hourly WiFi and communication provisions in your contract, which are vital (to communicate with your agent and family) in a remote location shoot?

All these things can be written into a contract or added on in additional pages called a 'Rider'. Also, please do not ever sign any contract that is not written in English. This may seem awful silly to say, but there are many horror stories of very young and trusting actors doing this. Even if someone you trust sits and translates it for you word for word, do not sign it. Get the contract written in your preferred language and get a copy of it. If they cannot provide that, then chances are that they will not provide anything written in that actual contract.

Do not ever be so grateful or desperate for the work that you do not think and then make these above mistakes. However, you do have to know what to look for and when and how to ask to have things written in. The lower the budget for the film the less you will find all these needed things. That does not mean you should not sign the contract, but you need to be very clear about what you are committing to, what you are not committing to, and what else you might need so that it can be put in or added on in a Rider so that you feel very good about signing it and your rights are protected. Your health and personal safety are always first and foremost. Double-check all your contracts, whether for stage or film.

Non-disclosure Agreements

A NDA is a very different kind of contract that actors often are asked to sign without even having a part in something. It means a non-disclosure agreement. Non-disclosure agreements are contracts as well and are very important. Sometimes you may sign them even for a new pilot audition or a small student film or independent film. Non-disclosure agreements protect not only the text and scene you are using to audition with or film, but also often the actual intellectual property, thoughts and ideas, as well. Non-disclosure agreements are meant to keep you silent about new projects, new episodes, new series and new films, and so respect them as well. They are meant very seriously, and you will be in deep trouble if you violate one by blabbing to your friends on your phone about your audition or a possible contract in something new, so after you do sign one keep your lips zipped about the text, the show and even the ideas, even if it is 'just' for an initial audition.

Very worth mentioning is that NDAs have also been used in the past by Harvey Weinstein and others in the entertainment industry in a very different way and that has been to buy the silence of young actresses. Being paid to sign a NDA rather than to tell on someone in power is something I hope none of you ever have to deal with. With the #MeToo movement the hope is that now NDAs will only be used to protect scripts and spoilers, not sexual predators.

You can contractually set things as you like a great deal of the time even on theatrical tours. I have a dear college friend who has travelled the world playing Pumba in *The Lion King* and he opts to travel from performance site to performance site in his own car when he is on the US tour legs, as opposed to travelling on the tour bus itself all the time. The peace of driving through the US centers him and keeps him much more relaxed for the shows. You can negotiate a lot of issues like this in your own contracts. However, always be sure that you have a way out of a longer term one or that at least you understand the full extent of whatever you sign – not that you ever want a way out of a contract, but most working actors make sure they know what the 'out' is in any contract they sign if they need to use it.

The Unions

When, how and what does it mean to join the performing unions? It means that your career and work have some protection, benefits, etc., but more importantly it means you are developed as an actor, much more professional and able to handle the competition. It also means you must do *no* non-union work. By the time you do go union make sure you are worth what they must spend to hire you. Be sure you have a sizeable and competitive resume if you are joining the union.

Be ready to compete, both with your resume and mentally and emotionally. Be ready for a higher stress level at auditions. Be ready for no more general calls (they are now called EPAs); now you get to have appointments you sign up for or that your agent sets. Be ready for things to be a bit more complicated with contracts. Be ready to possibly book less work due to competition from notable talent. Everything, from structured auditions and appointments to rehearsal rules, is stricter when you are union, but it offers a greater protection that most actors do not have in their regular life. Your life and work as an actor will be more complicated and challenging and wonderful once you are in the performing unions. Be well prepared with your acting credits and your idea of how to be professional when you join them.

When you do sign a contract you are then automatically a union actor, right? Not exactly. There are many non-union contracts being signed every day, both for film and stage. Many things you may think would be union are not – things like new media shows or improvisational streamed series on YouTube. These soon may be under union contracts, though. You may even be involved in a project that is 'signatory' with SAG-AFTRA, which means it adheres to all the union rules even if it does not fully contract with the union or pay union wages and benefits. You still may not be union, but if the project is signatory with SAG-AFTRA you are under their protection and jurisdiction. Even if you are signing a non union contract you can use these tips. Keep your eyes also on clauses about what happens if the project goes from non union to union status (as sometimes happens), or if it gets distributed overseas or online, or if your image or parts of the film or play are used in games or in other media, etc. You can insert, or ask for, union language in non union contracts in the form of Riders, attachments with additional clauses or points for your protection. Even if the contract is a non union one you can do this.

Most of the time when actors are trying to see the red flags in contracts the best bet is to be on the lookout for what is missing, not necessarily what is actually there. Another big red flag is when you ask the contract provider about something missing or something that feels wrong (such as reading about them having international rights to your image and likeness in a clause when you have not agreed to that and it is a domestic contract) and the answer is defensive and angry. People who are trying to cheat you will be defensive and angry or will dismiss your questions as nonsense or tell you not to worry about it. Trust me, worry about it. With the advent of the internet, illegally using actors' images and voices is easier to do internationally and much harder for an actor to track, so be on the lookout at all times. If you are in doubt about a contract or certain wording in a contract, go and ask a teacher, acting coach, lawyer, another agent or producer or a union actor (if you are not union) to have a look at a contract before you sign it. Call the unions themselves and ask them questions. You do not have to be a union member in order to call the union and ask them a question.

Sometimes signing a contract will get you a union card. Sometimes it will not. Do not ever despair. There are many 'backdoor' ways to join all the unions. For most actors there are really only two unions, AEA (for stage) and SAG-AFTRA (for everything else). A great way into AEA is TYA. TYA (Theater for Young Audiences) is well known for taking non union actors and offering them their first union contracts. You can also join AEA or SAG-AFTRA by virtue of working under a smaller sister union such as the American Guild of Variety Artists (AGVA) or American Guild of Musical Artists (AGMA) and having a union contract with them as a main entertainer. Hang on to that union contract for one year, pay your dues in that smaller union, and then walk into AEA or SAG-AFTRA after that one year and join the larger union. The same thing applies if you are either AEA or SAG-AFTRA and you want to join the other union. The contract that you joined AEA with will get you into SAG-AFTRA a year later (as long as dues are paid up) and vice-versa. Work one contract with SAG-AFTRA, wait a whole year and then you can join AEA and vice versa. However, join the union on that one year date or very shortly thereafter. Do not wait for one year and one month after you signed an AEA contract to go and join SAG-AFTRA, because it will be too late. Many actors surprisingly do not know about all this!

Does being union then change the process of you getting roles? It does indeed at times and certainly it changes the level of competition for them. Also, you cannot do non union work once you are a union member. That means not even a low budget non union web series –

nope, no way, nothing that is not union. Can you take a union leave of absence for a time to go do other non union work? Sure, but that non union job had better be the most life-changing and great part for you to want to leave the acting union for six months to a year to do it. More and more work is falling into union jurisdiction, even voice and streaming, web and digital work. When you do join the union, be ready to compete and truly work in the union, not to take a leave. If you are continually wanting to leave the union in order to work in many non union projects then the unions may not be the right choice for you.

Working in the Unions

Should you be a member of the union and try to fly under the union radar while still doing a non union role? I get asked this more often than I would like. The best answer is no. Not at all. If your doing non union work is so very important to you that you want to risk being caught and removed from the union for life (if you are caught, you will never be in that union again), then leave the union for good and do the non union work only. You cannot take continual union leaves – really, you can only request one or maybe two in your acting career. You can have a good career and even make some money and still continue to be non union. However, once you are a union member, either really commit to it or leave the union. Do not fart around.

All across the US there are showcase codes and developmental contracts for stage actors where union actors can work while still under the union banner. There are low budget and even ultra low budget contracts for actors to work under in film and TV while still being in the union jurisdiction. Even all voice over work that is union is under SAG-AFTRA jurisdiction or can be signatory with a union. AFTRA was the union for television and radio artists so it continues to cover all voice work and contracting that is union. Even if an actor is not in the union, the actor's contract may be union, or the project may go from non union to union status during production. Either way the unions will help with any issues and once you are in them it is wise to remain under that union banner.

If you're a union actor and you like making money shooting shows and working, know that the greatest threats to actors' livelihoods are

not non-union actors – it is SAG-AFTRA and AEA union member
actors who are sneakily working non-union jobs. These individuals
undermine the gains so many have sacrificed and fought for over
decades. The number one thing we as a union member should do
is to support and fortify our unions – not just the actors' union, but
all unions. When you work off the union card, you actively break the
unions down. You also let casting folks know they now can get union
members to work in non union jobs. That costs the union work,
money and contracts, and undermines you and your fellow actors
getting future work.

Actors should also be aware of a great group called Volunteer
Lawyers for the Arts (VLA). It was originally founded in New York
City and now has over fifty-three offices in the United States and
Canada. They give free legal advice to artists in dire financial need and
charge a small fee to others. They also serve non-profit arts groups for
free if they cannot afford it. If you do have some money then you
may be asked to pay some small administrative fees, but this helps out
other artists in the end. They can also offer advice on contracts, yearly
taxes and deductions for artists and non profit performing arts groups.
Their contact information will be in the last section of this book.

A last few words on contracts. We all have gut instincts – please
pay attention to and trust yours. If you have some doubts at all about
what you are signing, that is when you do not sign the contract. Ask
to take it home with you, for twenty-four or forty-eight hours of time
to review it. Then take it to someone you trust and ask them for help.
If someone hands you a contract and does not want you to review it,
then do not sign it. If they try to make you feel bad for even asking
questions about it, then do not sign it. If you are considering signing
a contract to go film in a war torn country where Ebola and rebel
guerrilla groups are prevalent and there is no contract provision for
medical or other evacuations, then do not sign it. If they threaten you
with, 'You had better sign it right now or the role goes to someone
else', then do not sign it. Do you really want to go work with the
people who do not even want to let you read the contract? Do you
want to work with the type of people who have made no provisions
to protect the actors in their film? No. If you think something is
wrong, then you are right in that feeling and do not sign that contract.
Trust your gut. Always.

15

FURTHER ARTISTIC CAREER OPTIONS IN THE NEW CENTURY WITH NEW TECHNOLOGY

I think that if you say this line at this particular point, we can get another laugh.

> The legendary Alfred Lunt, after two years of
> performing on stage in *O Mistress Mine* – now
> that is keeping it live!

I had a play, *Attitudes and the Dance*, produced! This was my big moment to shine, as actor and writer. I was proud of the work I spend months laboring over. Well, the play didn't unfold correctly. I had many problems I didn't know how to handle: I had unruly, lazy actors whose egos were bigger than their talent and a director afraid of confrontation. Needless to say, the production fell completely apart, got horrific reviews, and broke my desire to act. I thought I would never, ever get on stage again; I was mortally mortified, shocked, and hurt. If I had had my way (will), I would have withdrawn from the world to write and teach, never to feel the heat of spotlights again! End of career. But thank God, the world had other plans and ideas and dreams for me. My friend told me he was going to an audition, and before he went, I half-jokingly remarked, "If they need any drag queens, give them my number." And off he went only later to call me from the audition. "Stephen, you have to audition! This part is made for you! I'll drive you there." And I remember wanting to waffle and say, "I don't know . . ." But I said, "Yes." I remember putting on makeup and showing up at the audition. I busted through the door and said in my Bette Davis voice, "Where's the director?!"

I immediately began to work (own!) the room. I did a monologue from my show that bombed (this time all the humor and pathos were miraculously there). I read the sides, flirted with the producers, and I got the role. The new show, *It Started with a Lie,* was mounted on the exact same stage where I had "bombed," and I got some rave reviews and huge applause each night. See, all the things that I had learned and practiced had sharpened me, and I had the one magic element: willingness.

From *Awakening the Actor Within* by
C. Stephen Foster

Endless Opportunities

The world of entertainment, whether on stage or on film or in TV or in voice work or anywhere, is filled with endless opportunities for work and the absolute diversification of your career. Besides the motion capture work mentioned, actors who are athletes should be looking further at martial arts films, body doubling and even stunt work. If you look and present as very athletic then take advantage of all that to expand your career horizons. Get the training for stunt work, though – do not ever fake it. There are fabulous training facilities all across the country and some are listed in the back of this book. Faking knowing stunts will not get you the work as, if you have not been trained correctly or do not have some sort of knowledge base, they will not even insure you on the set to do the stunts. Danny Maze is a name you should know well if you want to get into stunts. Danny got his start in stunt gigs by being trained and then posting videos of himself on Instagram doing the stunts he had designed himself. His stunts and his talent got him tons of followers online, which then got him an agent, and now he is one of the top stuntmen in Hollywood. He literally created his own career.

Stunt Work

Another avenue for the physically inclined (and this does not mean only physically abled – I urge any disabled artists who are physically active to follow this and any other career paths as well) is to study stage combat, weaponry, martial arts and even fight directing, and to become combat certified so that you can become an actor who is also a fight director. This is another sideline of work that I have done at times, and it is very rewarding. You may then even be able to travel and stage fights all over the world, and often you can transition into staging fights for film or TV projects as well. There is an organized group you can join as you begin to work a lot in this field: the SDC, the Society for Stage Directors and Choreographers.

The field of audio book recording we have talked about: it has become much more than just a hobby for housewives or bored motorists to listen to and now is an international and global multi million dollar industry, being recorded around the world in a variety of languages. This is one of the fastest growing freelance markets for actors around. Most audio books nowadays are not recorded by celebrities in studios anymore, and actors who not only enter this market, but who are also able to learn how to record and engineer from their self-made home studios, are at the forefront of the trend and the money that funds it. The trend is that, I predict, 90 percent or more of global audio book work will be done by freelancers by 2020 and they will all work remotely and engineer their own audiobooks from their in home studios.

Jingles and Singing

Voice work opportunities, aside from reading and recording audio books, also include additional dialogue recording, backup singing for bands and other singers and also jingle singing. Jingles are the songs in commercials and on the radio; that field is as competitive as any voice field, but a good demo reel of your singing clips can get you started. Radio is still a booming place to find work as well, as is its sister field of online podcasts. Many actors think live radio is failing due to podcasts and the like, but it is not and remains a real viable option in voice announcing, disk jockeying (DJing), jingle singing and commercial voice over work.

Stand-ins and Body Doubles

Actors can also do stand-in or body doubling work, which is where you have the same height and build and even look of an actor who is well known and who does not want to expend their energy standing under hot lights while the lights are being focused. So you stand under the hot lights for them, and often you then get not only a paycheck and some on set experience, networking, benefits and a pension plan, but also often you get lines in the show and some good career contacts. Most actors I know who have worked as stand-ins or doubles make great money, get some small parts on that show and build a good career with a show on TV. Many well known actors have begun their career as stand-ins.

Internationally

On the international front of voice work the growing dubbing and looping market is one all actors would do well to get involved in. International television shows are now being brought straight to the United States via Hulu, Amazon and Netflix, and are often not being refilmed with American actors in the roles, but are instead being entirely dubbed with American voices and dialogue instead. If you are already in the voice over market you will be on the ground floor for finding and auditioning for this work. These opportunities will come in via your agent or via the websites like Actors Access that you use as casting platforms, both for voice acting and also for live acting.

Print and Parts Modeling

Print work is also something that most actors will encounter at some point in their career as they may be offered a catalogue photo shoot gig, or an ad for some product, but there is the also the unique, quirky and wonderful world of print work in part modeling (hands, feet, chests, torso, neck, legs, and even body doubling for nude work in films), which can make you very lovely money and not impact your acting career at all (nobody will know, unless you tell them, that your feet are the ones in the Skechers shoe ad or that your hands are the ones in the new Swarovski crystal ad). Your butt could be a naked stand-in butt for Reese Witherspoon and nobody will ever know.

The main requirement for this parts modeling field is that, male or female, you have to have the average size hand or foot that the United

States has if you do shoes or gloves modeling. You want to be able to model the glove or shoe easily, so you need to be the average size. If you have delectable shoulders or a unique neck that can also earn you money. Not only can being a 'parts' model be very lucrative, at $2,000–5,000 a day per job, but very often you get to keep many of the items that you have modeled. I have a gal pal who has spent many years doing foot modeling, as she has the perfect size seven foot, and she must have 300 pairs of shoes. I have another pal, a gorgeous, unique and bald actress/model, who has done the cover of *Time* magazine as they used the back of her neck and head to plug a computer cable into for a cover photo about technology. Part modeling is just that, about parts, not about being gorgeous. It is often about being unique, not model-y. You may be fifty pounds overweight and have a broken nose, but if that nose is unique you could model it. Places to start in all of these modeling areas are in the resources section at the end of the book. The possibilities for you are endless.

Do it Yourself

Self-generated projects for stage and film, TV and online work are also the wave of the future. You can create your own new web series today and let it take off online. It does not even have to be a live action project with live actors. Perhaps you have a friend who is an accomplished animator. She then draws the characters while you do the voices, and you both create a new YouTube series. Web series are often great fun and frequently now are being bought up entirely, repackaged for publicity and marketing, and shown on Hulu and other major providers as new shows. Even in live auditions for web series it usually will require loads of fun improvisation work, so if you are an actor who can think on your feet and improvise then start putting that good stuff you come up with on paper. YouTube videos and web series are also now taking off and are making their stars millions. You should be thinking about how to create and market yourself as an actor – why not also think about how to market your own creative work as well? Why not write and film and create your own projects? These projects do not even have to be about acting or have any performance angle. Perhaps you groom dogs as a hobby, build something around that. Maybe you cook, sing, dance, or you can talk about the weather. Put your own personal spin on it and it may take off. Any idea in the world can work if it is fun and appealing and you enjoy doing it.

If you are very technically computer savvy why not create and edit reels (both video and audio reels) and media for other performers? If you are good with text and writing, why not have a resume business or do freelance writing jobs? Think outside the box. You do not have to spend a ton of money to learn new technical skills as well. You can teach yourself to work with iMovie, Sony Vegas products, Adobe and .pdf files, Audacity and recording and editing voice clips, Quicktime and movies and more. Being self taught does not mean you are not at a professional level. If you are a member of SAG-AFTRA you can attend their computer labs as often as you wish and learn everything from creating a web series to editing and filming techniques, all because of your union membership.

Teaching yourself to work with different kinds of software opens up new possibilities. Create your own vocaloids and do your own commercials with them. Think outside the box? In reality, there is no box at all. None. Not anymore. Not like there was twenty years ago. With technology changing and the global entertainment industry changing so rapidly now, there is no limit to what you can create and market. Maybe you will be the one actor to create the next big thing in the world of entertainment, and it may be something nobody has even thought of yet.

Trends to Come

A trend that I can certainly foresee being something to capitalize on is in the future market for smaller and shorter segmented episodes of web series or YouTube series, my guess is anywhere from six to eight or ten minutes long, geared to a more 'I want it now' and a much shorter attention spanned world. Another future trend I see could be an increase in the user end (the buyers of video games) technology of video game gear – glasses, gloves, special helmets, shoes and plastic or lightweight 'weapons', and who knows what type of future other wearables, which could then be purchased to add to and enhance the buyer's interaction with their video games, TV and home theater film viewing. Any way you can think of to take advantage of this and get on board these possible trends can work for you, make you money and give you some artistic freedom.

Add into this new eclectic media mix all of the existing secondary options for actors, such as directing, choreography, video production, screenplay writing, modeling of all kinds, casting and producing, and all the other myriad of things that already exist as sidelines for actors. You have a variety of ways to not only enrich and practise your craft, but to keep cash flowing and yourself competitive and creative in a rapidly changing technologically heavy world. The fact that many of these things can be your own at home 'day job' work while you are in between films or stage jobs makes it even better. You can begin to plan when and where and how you work (and sometimes even who you work with). You can begin to have multiple revenue streams from audiobooks, some residuals or a YouTube channel (which can be 'monetized' by letting advertisers put ads on it that your subscribers watch and you then get paid for, etc.) that you can start to rely on to pay your bills every month. Artists who are lucky enough to be artists their whole life do so in part because they make a lot of different kinds of art and they create things that work for them and bring in multiple income streams. They often are able to pick the jobs they want within the exact time frames they need and to literally create the artist life they want.

Are all of these not enough ideas for you yet? What about you creating and acting in your very own one man or one woman show on stage? There are 'solo' festivals all over the world that constantly look for one person shows to come and perform in them. What about creating your own cabaret act? You can sing and dance and tell the audience about your life. What about you doing stand-up comedy? It is still huge as a career sideline and any comedy club in the country has an open mic night every single week. If you go in, get yourself up, do a few minutes and be truly funny and hip and current – trust me, you will get that foot in the comedy door and be asked to come back. You can do acting work in theme parks (why not be the prince in *Aladdin* for a year or so and bank the money?) and on cruise ships too.

Especially if you are young and unattached (no pets, spouses or kids), why not spend six months or a year cruising around the world doing a show and getting a paycheck, benefits and a union card?

I have a dear friend on a cruise ship at this very moment in *Priscilla Queen of the Desert* and she is having the time of her life, getting paid good money, getting free room and board, travelling and singing, dancing and acting. She is getting paid to cruise around the world and sing, dance and act. It is also a great credit on her actor resume and the role she played will carry good cache with many casting directors in her future.

If you truly are an artist and actor then go out and do it. Perform in museums, in barns, on the street, in stadiums, at parties, on boats, in hospitals, in prisons, doing dinner theater in restaurants in Idaho, or wherever you can. Perform in the National Parks doing shows about people who have influenced nature, perform historic roles during museum tours. Everything is a potential way to enlarge your own talent and grow your own career. There is a company in New York City who will bring three actors to your apartment and perform a small and intimate play for you and your three dinner guests. In your apartment, literally theater on demand in your home. I have personally performed in prisons, hospitals, parks, festivals and at private parties and many other places, too many to recount. Keep your eyes open for all opportunities and keep your mind alert to possibilities for your career.

16

ACTORS OF COLOR, THOSE WITH DISABILITIES, THOSE IN THE LGBTQIA COMMUNITY

When representation is only making fun of disabled people or asking little people to bite someone's butt or disabled people having to ask for permission to get the opportunity to get a job, then clearly there is a little bit of human rights abuses going on.

Orlando Jones

The 2017 Primetime Television Emmy Awards, regardless of the 2016 election and the political issues surrounding it, were probably the most inclusive in television history in the pool of winners with people of color, women and LGBTQIA folks taking home many awards. The 2018 Oscar pool is doing well also, with actors of color and a female cinematographer nominated. You will note that I did not mention any disabled artists, however – there is much work still to be done in Hollywood. The era of white male dominance in Hollywood, whether behind the scenes, in the casting area or on camera, is now crumbling (especially in light of the 2017 sexual scandals and the #MeToo movement) and more artists of color, women, gay and transgender artists, and artists with disabilities are now coming to the forefront. With newer generations coming in and younger directors and casting people taking over in Hollywood in the next ten years or so, this will become even more diversified. This is a much needed trend in the arts that will continue for all of these marginalized groups in entertainment.

Disabled Representation

Yet, in early 2018, Alec Baldwin (playing a blind man) and Jake Gyllenhaal (playing a bomb victim who loses his legs) and Andrew

Garfield (playing a man with polio) and Joaquin Phoenix (playing a paralyzed cartoonist) and Hong Chau (playing a woman missing part of a leg) and Sally Hawkins (playing a mute woman) and Denzel Washington (playing a role arguably on the autism spectrum), and quite a few other actors still, will all play disabled lead roles in major motion pictures coming from Hollywood. Hollywood is openly talking about disability quite a lot now, yes, but it is not doing even remotely enough about casting it and pursuing true representation of it in film. Hollywood is paying a lot of lip service to the idea instead of creating any change. The actors are out there, the very well trained disabled actors who should be auditioning for these above films; Hollywood is simply not manning up and casting them and, in too many cases, not even auditioning them. That will change.

Disability representation is the most important in Hollywood because it is the least talked about and dealt with. The future trend, whether Hollywood likes it or not, will be to start to reward real representation (the TV show *Speechless* comes to mind) on TV and in film and to slowly do away with the Oscar and Golden Globe nominations for actors who 'play' disabled. Would Hollywood put forth Andrew Garfield to play a black man? Would they cast Emma Stone as an Asian? (Well, yes, they stupidly did and that film failed.) If Hollywood is headed towards no 'whitewashing' of roles, they need to also head towards no 'cripping up' of roles as well. I predict none of the actors I mentioned at the start of this paragraph wins an Oscar in 2018. The disabled artists are done seeing able-bodied actors playing disabled roles. They now will begin to use even more voting, purchasing and political power to change that. No more whitewashing, no more cripping up. That is one trend that is coming to an end within the next decade or even sooner.

All I wanted for Christmas was to see reviews of #Downsizing question why no #amputee actors were seen. When I lost my leg I never dreamed how differently I'd be treated, even though I'm still the same person, and a much better #actor. Anyone can become disabled at any time but no one cares that people with disabilities never get the opportunities that their able-bodied peers receive. Shouldn't THAT scare you more than actually becoming disabled? Time to stop treating people with disabilities like we're second class citizens, only here to be pitied or to inspire. So much for equal opportunity.

Rachel Handler, actress, writer, singer and advocate

Trends in the Work You Can Use

What are the trends in the arts as a whole that you as a non-white male can capitalize on to get more substantial work? If you are a disabled artist, something that is often forgotten is letting casting people know how you can work in various mobility settings. If you can use that to your advantage and simply note it on your resume ("I can perform walking slowly, using a cane, using arm crutches or utilizing a wheelchair", or you may say you will perform with or without your prosthetic arm or leg), it can not only help to get you work, but also can often open a casting director's mind and relax them into talking about things they may feel uncomfortable about asking you about your potential. Help out these casting directors by letting them know the physicalities your body can work in comfortably. Often they may want to enquire about a physical mobility issue as they are thinking of casting you, but they simply do not have the vocabulary or comfort zone to address it. Often when a casting person is unable to address this issue, their own frustration leads them to dismiss the disabled actor. You then can be the one to open that discussion if you are in the mental and emotional place to do so.

If you are lucky enough to be biracial or of a mixed heritage use that to your advantage and take a moment to understand the many nationalities you can possibly look like (you might not only look black or Asian or simply an undefined biracial person, but you might also look Moroccan, Egyptian, Arabic, Italian, Basque, Lithuanian, Russian and much more). Think outside the box in regard to your own potential appearance (and in regard to your acting clips on your reel so you can show us different nationalities in those). If you do look like six or seven different races, be certain to learn those accents, if it feels comfortable to you, so you can audition for roles of those races. With globalization of casting it no longer matters if you are a certain race exactly (which was a very big deal years ago) – now, it is just that you can look like it. Those casting people actively casting people of color are often willing to cast across lines (an Asian woman playing an

Egyptian princess, for instance) if you are willing and able to do it. The conflicts come when white actors play all the roles, not when actors of color are allowed to work.

Note, if you speak ASL, many actors who are CODAs (children of deaf parents) or who are at a solid level of fluency in ASL never put it on their resume. Do so. It is a language and, if you speak it, then say so. How else will the casting directors ever know? You must defy all their ingrained ideas about disabled artists or artists of color by giving them solid information that opens their brains and then stunning them in auditions.

Twenty years ago, around this same time in the morning, I had the surgery that changed my life forever. My right leg was taken off, and turned around (in various pieces), leaving my weak, left, CP-ridden leg to do the rest of the work. It would take me around two years to completely learn to walk again. Twenty years ago today, around this time, my Dad went to the CVS downstairs in the hospital and bought nearly every magazine with Leonardo DiCaprio's face on the cover so I'd have something nice to look at as I went under anesthesia. I was missing the opening weekend of *Titanic*. I would name my wheelchair Leonardo DiCaprio so I could sit in his lap. Twenty years ago today, I woke up from that surgery, my mother's face was the first one I saw. I started crying because I wasn't sure what was going on, I forgot what happened, and I wanted to walk but couldn't. Almost twenty years later, I wrote a solo show about it. It premiered in 2016 at Solocom in NY and I took it back to Boston in 2017. I have had the busiest year of my professional acting career (with jobs on three major TV shows) with more to come. I have yet to meet Leonardo DiCaprio. But I learned to walk again, so anything is possible.

Stephanie Salvato Gould, actress, writer

Access to Everything for all Actors

Physical access is vital for any disabled artist and is something that often nobody else thinks about, but you must know what to do if you do not get it. If you cannot get into a building to audition, you do need to call (your agent, the casting director or whoever set up the audition) and complain about it. Ask about coattail access, even (coattail access is being able to enter a building via a freight elevator or another way normally not meant for usual access), which, although not the best access, will still get you into the building and auditioning. Of course, if you have been set to audition for a disabled role, you will have usually have guaranteed access (although not always) to the audition space – but what about when you audition for a non-disabled role?

First, you must get yourself to start auditioning for any and every role that interests you – do not let anyone limit your auditioning and do not do it yourself. Nobody should limit you. Not an agent, not a manager, not friends, not family members. Then, once you get out there actively auditioning, you can begin to tackle access or the lack of it. I always advise disabled artists to submit for everything that interests them, no matter what. If it does not say, "Disabled artists should not apply" (and it will not ever say that), then apply for it all. Be the artist who changes their minds. This goes for actors of color as well. Submit for whatever you feel you are right for, no matter what color is requested; submit for everything you want to, break that glass ceiling.

So, how do you go about opening a casting director's mind? You must walk in and have worked so hard that you make them see you as an artist, not as a person with a disability or of a certain color or even a certain gender. No, it will not always work; sometimes you will even encounter confusion or anger, but it will work more now than in any other time in history. Think about that – never in history has there been a better time for people of color, women, LGBTQIA artists and disabled artists to show up and show off. How then can you be sure that you will get the same exact treatment, the same consideration for the role, as other actors? How can you be sure you get the same consideration as a white male? You can't. You never can, whether you have a disability or you are biracial or you are female or gay or straight or white or not. All you can do is show up and be so professional and prepared that you knock their socks off. Any way that you can get that audition and get in that room, get it. Show up, talk your way in and do your job and be brilliant. After that it is out of your hands, as it always is. Remember, there has never been a better time in stage or film history, *ever*, to be a different type of artist and shine. This is your moment.

How You Should Look

Be the distinct person that you are – in fact you should cultivate that. If you look different from others, then do so, and be proud. Be ugly, tall, heavy set, hairy, biracial, triracial; walk with a limp or have a cleft palate. You want to stand out, so do not blend in with everyone else and be forgotten easily. Choose a hairstyle that looks good on you, even if it is not the hottest thing around. Wear the clothes you like, have a distinct sense of your own style. Look like you. Be the you that is unforgettable.

"There's still a lot of misconceptions about who trans people are," *Orange is the New Black*'s Laverne Cox told the Television Critics Association. "There are so many representations of us being victims or predators," and "they influence the way in which policies are made, so it's so crucial that we have representations on television that are diverse, that represent the full humanity of trans people. We have to tell these stories better, because lives are on the line."

Intersectionality and spectrums of appearances in artists is a newer reality that one can use to your advantage. A gay, black, Jewish woman with one leg. It sounds like the punchline of a very rude joke. Yet, that is an example of one or more socially marginalized groups intersecting in one person (called intersectionality), and frequently now new roles and new projects are written in order to highlight that intersectionality. If intersectionality is within your acting profile, again be proud of it and work with it. Do not hide it. You will often have to teach casting people and educate others as you go, but it benefits us all.

What to Disclose

What things about yourself should an actor make an agent or casting director's business and when? You should disclose to a director if and when something on a set or a stage is a safety issue for you or someone else, if something is an access issue if you are disabled, if something is a medical need or an issue that puts you at risk, when something is a mental and emotional comfort issue, or an intimacy issue in 'those' physically intimate or physically violent scenes. Their business is to have any information that may affect the project or performer safety.

You may even have situations where you must weigh getting the work against your own personal safety (you want the job but are not sure you can do the wheelchair wheelie they want for the role without snapping your own spine) or your mental and emotional well being (you are a young black actor having real trouble processing a very physical racist lynching scene). I cannot make your job choices for you, but I can say for certain that there will always be an audition for you to go to. You, however, only have one body and mind, one special you. Cherish it. Stand up for it. Show it off. Also, be sure to protect it.

> That time I remember I was told that I couldn't be seen for My Fair Lady because I was Asian. And I had already won my Tony.
> Lea Salonga

What is not ever the casting director's, or even your agent's, business? Their business does not include your genitals or lack thereof, that you are trying to get pregnant, that you currently are pregnant (if it does not affect the two day or two week shoot or impact your work), your future plans to move to a new agent in a month or a year, your sexual activities, your surgeries, your hormones, your lovers, your gender transition, your nationality, sexuality, racial or ethnic background, religion or lack thereof, your age, or your HIV status. They can ask about these things; however, *none* of that is anyone's business except yours. Your personal issues (and this is particularly true for the LGBTQIA community where some outside that community often may feel too free to ask about surgeries or genitals) are not their business. You may, even as a young and very new actor, say, "I'm sorry, but that has no impact on this work and is inappropriate." You can build your new reputation as someone who is not a pushover. Stand up for yourself even if it means giving up a role or walking out of an audition calmly and politely. In the long run you will be glad you did this for so many reasons, one of which will be your own ethical beliefs and being true to them. Being a polite artist does not mean you must allow people into your personal life or that you must become a doormat in order to get or keep a role. Keep your personal space your own.

Unfortunately, if you are disabled, in the LGBTQIA spectrum or a person of color you end up being an involuntary ambassador for those artists who come after you. That has usually been the case in history and it continues to be so now. You also unfortunately become an involuntary educator. Neither is a job you signed up for, you just want to be an actor! However, every time you are clear, calm and proud about who you are, and what your talent is and is not, and what you will or will not put up with, you pave the way for others who are different to follow you and for the busy casting staff or agents to get their rude or naive assumptions in check. You will also sometimes encounter pushback from other actors (usually white actors, and I say that being a white actor) who are very nervous about people of color, gender fluid artists and disabled artists now in competition with them for roles. These actors like the fact that they are white and the most castable. They do not want their bubbles burst. But, burst those bubbles will be. Educate them if you care to and, if not, you owe them nothing except politeness. You are an actor − do not feel you must justify your acting or your own uniqueness to anyone.

Imperfection

Being imperfect is what I always look for when I cast actors and whether they admit it or not that is what all casting directors and agents look for. I once taught a pretty large acting seminar where the participants each got to present a monologue. One of the actors, a handsome young fellow, began his monologue and about half way through it he got the oddest look on his face but he kept on talking. When he finished I asked him what was going on? Whatever it was, it completely took over the monologue and was all that we were interested in − not his acting. He said that he had had a nose itch during the monologue and that it drove him nuts. Aghast, I asked him why he did not scratch his nose. "Well, I didn't want to mess up the monologue. I wanted it to be perfect," he said. Sigh.

Mess it up. *Please.* Keep it live and real. Wipe your nose, burp − if you have an itch, for goodness' sake, scratch it. You would in real life. Be different and unique and real. If you do not scratch your nose then you look odd; if you try to hide your uniqueness you appear fake; and we then lose all real interest in your acting because we focus on your looking odd or fake. Acting and imperfections are a reflection of reality. Especially for the LGBTQIA community, disabled artists and actors of color, play to your beautiful imperfections, embrace your gorgeous differences. They are your strengths in the casting room.

17

YOU AS AN ARTIST IN THE MIDST OF CHANGING TECHNOLOGY

Talent is not definable, but it is very recognizable.

Anonymous

The additional tools, besides all the audition work and practice and coaches and teachers and classes and seminars, that you can use to get ahead in the entertainment world are networking (and more networking), learning all about computers and film and theatrical technology, and really building up a stellar reputation of both your work and your impeccable work ethics. When you go an entire year in a career and do three films, two plays, direct another play and do fight direction for another show, do three audiobooks and then realize you have not had to audition or interview for any of it, then you know your reputation is working for you. Then you know you are getting offered work simply on the strength of your reputation and the work itself. They already know the product that you will provide is good.

Maintaining Yourself

This also helps you in the everyday maintenance of yourself as an artist, as, if you are not stressed out about your developing reputation or fixing bad situations you have caused, then you can carry yourself everywhere with confidence and can be much more stunning, relaxed and real in auditions. We, as artists, are responsible for creating work that will hopefully help our society to evolve and that will even help each other. Yet we always seem to forget to do the same helping things for ourselves as artists, with self care an ignored option in our lives. Care for yourself, both your reputation as an artist and as a person.

I also cannot ever say enough about networking as an actor. Most – not all, but most – roles for films and productions and even seasons of television are cast because people cast actors whom they know and like. Often things are cast with no auditions at all. I know I have myself cast smaller shows or projects with no auditions. It is rare, but I have done it. Get to know everyone that you can in your city; see films and plays and go meet the people in them. Go backstage and tell other actors you like their work. Talk to the director. See films and stay for the discussion session afterward. Every one of those people you meet is a contact. The old man sweeping the floor at the theater is a contact, the secretary and the audition monitor is a contact. Meet everyone you can, and get to know everyone you can. This is networking. It also helps to be free and single as you can attend more things and go to more places, but if you are not single be sure to have an understanding partner who also loves being social. You will need a great partner, as the life of an actor is a tough one.

Training in a Digital World

If you are a young actor about to choose a college or a specialized course of study, look for one that incorporates more of both film and theater schools, that has a green or blue screen room on campus, that allows for study in all fields. If you do opt to study theater, take a film class or six as well. If you are studying film acting take theater classes and delve into Shakespeare. California Institute of the Arts is one such place that feeds all options, and New York University is another; they both support study of theater as well as acting in some student films. Start building the resume and knowledge banks you need even while you are still in college. Get to know the film students on your campus well because they will be the very same ones making the Hollywood films five years after you all graduate. Get both stage experience and on set experience if you can before you leave any school and have to enter a more competitive world. If you do all this before you graduate, you will graduate feeling more secure about your talent.

Business is Where Actors Often Fail

Acting is an art, but it is also a business and actors who do not see this, or who ignore it, do so at their own peril. Being a business person is something you must also become and treating yourself, in whatever field or guise, as a business means always being on the lookout for how to make your business work better. Did you take an on-camera class about commercial auditions? Where are the clips of your work in that class? Did you take an acting workshop and, if so, was it then filmed? Where are the clips of the three student films you did last year? Get clips of everything possible; keep business cards from everyone you meet; keep receipts from what you buy; and keep your reel as updated and fluid as you can. Gently nag the filmmakers you work with and remind them that their work gets further exposure in your reel and on your website, but only if they remember to send you the actual film clips. Many times during the editing process of a film you can get clips they know they will not even use in the final film, but only if you ask for them and then ask again. Then politely ask some more until you get them.

Be in constant control of your actor website, your acting and voice reels (you can even create them yourself and then edit them and keep your own reels updated) as they are the main tools in your toolbox showing how you are presented to the world as an actor. Do not ever share your passwords – always protect your image and likeness and your future career. Reels are vital to you. What do casting people look for in your reels, then? In general we want to see a variety of clips, lighting, angles of shots, hair, beards and more looks from you that inspire us to cast you in many roles. You should have a good clip (a hero or good guy), a meth head or scarier clip, an attorney or surgeon, a doofus goofing off, a dramatic scene, a funny one, a clip with a child if you could play a parent, a clip with a person of the opposite sex, or the same sex if you are an out gay artist. If you can appear to be various nationalities or can do accents, we need to see at least one, if not two, clips of you doing some accent or as some other nationality. We need to see full body clips, close ups and everything in between. We need everything that you can possibly be cast as, but in just about two minutes only. We can see it in four minutes if you have two reels, one comedy and one drama. We need to see all the facets of the diamond that you are so that we can think of, or be made aware of, a variety of roles to cast you in.

Another very important issue in regard to your own public relations and how you present yourself to the world is the following item. Whether you sign NDAs or not, *do not* ever post your own callsheets, contracts, cast lists, on set pictures or anything like this before your episode of whatever show it is airs. If you do this, you are most likely violating NDAs and you are posting other people's personal information as well within those cast lists. Most agents and managers will drop you if you do this constantly. If I see that a young actor who perhaps has booked a show like *Bull* and a few other small parts and that they have posted their call sheet online (with the names of every other actor working in that episode, some of whom have signed NDAs and do not want their names public) as well as on set pictures of other actors and even chunks of scripts or full cast lists with names of characters – wow. This is someone who is not only playing with fire in regard to contract breaking and NDA breaking, but this is also someone who appears very immature and slightly desperate for attention. This does not help advance your career or your reputation. You may get away with it for a few years, but it will catch up with you eventually. After your episode airs then you can do it, except for the posting of other actors' information online. In this information sharing age it is easy to forget, but do not get in the bad habit of oversharing and posting too much information online, especially when it is not your own information.

IMDb

Another word about all of those short films, student films or indie films that you do work on. Once you do work on one and it then gets accepted into any film festival anywhere, the director of that film can then make an entry on the Internet Movie Database (IMDb) for that film. IMDb is where you can find any working actor and their credits, along with their pictures and clips from films, interviews and so forth. Make sure that, as your films hit the festival circuit, you create your own actor page on IMDb so that all those film pages from your films can then be linked back to your IMDb page as well as any TV and theater credits you do too. When casting people look you up on the internet, you want to be sure to have an IMDb page. This is a sign that you are serious and it is as important as your social media activity is to your career.

Actors should always work at being actors. You should take classes, seminars, ask questions and gain knowledge, watch people and read. In what other ways can you think of planning for the future? Well, learn for yourself how to see coming trends (another one of which I predict will be is an increase in more 'political' theater on stage and in the public forum) and pay attention to how many more self tapes you send out this year than last, how many more location shoots do you do in six months, how many times have you been seen by the same casting person, how many times have you read for the same TV show, and so forth. If you can see and understand your own personal trends, you can then capitalize on them.

Some trends I can predict continuing, as well as the trend of greatly increased self taping of actors, are more social media activities for auditions (including audition notices on Facebook and Twitter, Instagram and maybe even Pinterest and MySpace), more self made newsletters and email lists going out from actors, more writing and self-production of all forms of media, more actors creating their own YouTube careers and sustainable incomes, and an overall upswing in actors writing, filming, casting, marketing and producing and even travelling with their own original work.

Why Were You Not Cast?

In addition, something else you must actively do (and this is really tough, I know) is to try to give up not knowing the reason you do not get cast. There is no way technology or even charting industry trends will help you figure this out. Ever. First, understand that you will rarely find out why you did not get cast in that role – you just will not. Worse than that, often the reason you did not get the role may be petty and stupid and something you have absolutely no control over. Many times it has nothing to do with your amazing acting at all. Countless times I have watched a casting director not cast an actor because they remind them of someone in their past that they hate (old college boyfriends or girlfriends are the top actor killers). Or they have the wrong hair. Or "I do not like his eyes". The actor has absolutely no control over this type of immature decision making and will never really know why they were not cast, so just try to let it go. Go in and do the best job you can with that audition on that day and leave proudly and move on to the next one.

Now, if your new acting or voice over career starts to get pretty busy, you should know that the only acceptable excuse to get out of a role, audition or a conflict is the one that I will tell you. Saying that your dog is sick, or that you have a dental appointment, may get you out of something at your 'day job' work so you can go to an audition, but they will be unhappy about it. The only halfway acceptable excuse in the industry itself for missing a rehearsal, getting out of a role you have committed to, or missing or rescheduling an audition is because of getting 'other acting work'. Within the industry, work is the only excuse for missing other work. In your day job you can tell your boss that you have a root canal, or that your aunt Mona died, in order for you to get to an audition. However, if you have an audition for a small but great role and then get another audition at the same time for a leading role, you can keep both auditions, but try to rearrange the first or second one simply by saying a past gig called and asked you to do some ADR during that same time period and can they reschedule? Or you just got a call from a prior audition and have to shoot something at the same time as their audition and could you instead audition earlier or later that day? Most likely they will reschedule you or move your times around. Why? Because, again, the only good excuse for rescheduling any work in this industry is other work in the industry. A secondary benefit of this lovely excuse is that it makes you sound like a busy, working actor and everyone always wants to work with the actor who is already busy working. Always do your very best to appear busy and hard at work.

Taxes

Since acting is a business (yes, of course it is art, but it is also a business and you should think of it that way), and you are a marketable product as an actor you are allowed to write off some tax deductions (at least in 2018 for 2017) for some acting expenses for the acting income you have earned. Consult your tax advisor about tax deductions and keep accurate records of all of your acting expenses. Get a great big jar and dump your receipts into it like mad all year long. And then take them out, add them up and use them at tax time. Many of these deductions will be lost if the new GOP tax plan really and finally goes into effect, so we can hope for the best for artists and that these deductions will continue. Possible tax deductions can include:

- travel expenses to and from your auditions (including meals and lodging, gas and some car maintenance)
- admissions to movies and plays you go to (save all your ticket stubs)
- acting classes, workshops and seminars you attend
- acting books and magazines, including this one
- office supplies as you work from your home on your career
- mailing expenses if you mail anything out
- telephone bills, including the cost of an answering machine or service, a pager, or cellular phone
- union dues if you are union
- headshots (photographers' fees and duplication costs)
- resume (printing and duplication costs)
- videotape and DVD rentals
- television set, VCR, DVD player, and the cost of your monthly cable subscription service
- makeup and clothing specifically used for acting or auditions (including any dry cleaning expenses)
- costs of creating and duplicating a demo tape if you put it on DVD
- membership to Actors Access, *Backstage* and IMDb
- voice classes, dance classes, commercial classes and any other performing classes.

As well, if any artists have the money they should buy these things as further deductibles. Here is a starter list of things you may want to purchase now and claim later in preparation for the taxation changes:

- movie pass
- print cartridges
- resume paper
- Fedex print/copy card
- postage

- envelopes
- markers, pens, pencils
- pre-pay Netflix, Hulu, Amazon Prime
- pre-pay Actors Access account, Casting Networks, *Backstage*, etc.
- pre-paid dance class card
- pre-pay lessons and coachings
- pre-pay web-hosting
- that new computer or tablet you've had your eye on
- phone charging cables
- new batch of headshot print-outs
- headshot session
- audition binder
- clear binder sleeves
- post-its
- printer
- Stage Write or other theater software
- components for your home voice over studio
- components for your "self tape" set up.
- pre-pay iTunes cloud service fee
- pre-pay any business related subscriptions, including periodicals, service agreements, storage and hosting
- stage manager supplies
- teaching supplies
- dressing room supplies
- your professional gifts of up to $25 per person (a thank you for your agent perhaps?)
- bus/train tickets for business travel you know is coming-up

Giving yourself as many tax deductibles as you can is vital for all artists. Also, give yourself as many artistic options as possible for your life (learning all kinds of audition techniques and auditioning for everything), as this means that not only will you be an artist in so many different ways, but also that you will have many times in your life where you can pick and choose the work you do and the tax deductions you get. When you are between TV gigs or film roles you will be busy doing audiobooks, painting or hand modeling or writing your own YouTube series. Do as much as you possibly can. The first few years will be rough, but after that you should be able to at least do sporadic work in a few fields and continue to keep the ball rolling into being a working artist.

Net Neutrality for Artists

The possible loss of net neutrality and what it means for artists and entertainment is still being debated; however, we can be certain it will be catastrophic for the online and video streaming entertainment world. Certainly it will impact the acting unions and earning potential; residuals collected by working actors; web series being produced, bought and sold; casting platforms, which may be hosted by companies now wanting actors to pay more to use them; viewing entertainment and films, and increased costs to do that. Netflix, Hulu, Amazon Prime and others will all be compromised, as will actor work, residuals and revenue. Actors all over the US will have to find workarounds for any net neutrality loss and casting directors and agents will have to do the same. If it happens it could be horrible, but actors are nothing if not persistent. Your career will find a way to flourish and grow, no matter what the restrictions are to come in 2018 and beyond. My prediction is that net neutrality will be talked about, yelled about, but that nothing will change. Have faith in that.

Further Questions I Get Asked by Aspiring Actors

What about tattoos? Should actors have them? Tattoos and whether to get them or not are a constant question young actors ask about – and they are now just fine to have in the new century. Gone are the days where no actor ever has any tattoos, or at least where they pretended not to; there are many kinds of makeup you can wear to cover them now. I have never seen a tattoo cost an actor or actress an acting job unless it was on their face. You can have tattoos on your face, of course, but know that you will then probably be cast as drug dealers, prison gang members and the like (unless, of course, you cover them up with makeup). If that limited casting potential works just fine for you, then tattoo that face! Body tattoos often do not even come into any film as they are on body parts not normally shown. I had a tattoo for years on the inside of my ankle and, if I happened to be cast in something where I wore shorts, I simply popped a bandaid over it.

Now I have a few tattoos and plan for more and don't even think about it twice. Makeup is your best friend.

What about scars? Can actors with scars find work? Scars are also fine for actors to have, but there is still a big double standard between men and women having them. Tommy Flanagan, a lovely Scottish actor, gets plenty of roles in TV and films although he has a Joker smile type scar on both sides of his face. Were he a woman in TV he would never be able to work without fully covering up the facial scars. Tina Fey, although her chin scar is small, is one of the more prominent females around with a facial scar who works in TV and film. This does not mean that you cannot become an actor working with an obvious scar. Go for it. Again there is nothing stopping you from breaking any barrier.

What about piercings? Any and all kinds of piercings? I get asked about piercings a lot as well. Camryn Manheim worked for years with ear piercings run wild and nobody cared. She and many male actors with pierced ears opened the floodgates for piercings and this is no longer taboo for actors. Facial piercings (such as cheeks and tongues) you may want to mull over, however, as this again relegates you to gang member and emo band roles. It sets the casting person up to typecast you at times unless you change their mind. Tongue piercings can be fine if you can be understood, and if they fit the role you are auditioning for or they are not obvious. If that is all fine with you as an actor, pierce away.

The casting I speak of when I talk about tattoos and piercings and the like is the mainstream film and TV casting. Indie films, experimental theater projects and the changing production landscape, and your own creative work may not care as much about piercings and tattoos. If you walk in and audition for *Hamlet*, and you do have facial piercings, I will cast you as Hamlet if you are the best actor for the role. Period. I do not let superficial things like that stop my casting a really good actor. However, I am known for casting in odd and new ways and mainstream casting most of the time does not cast like me.

What about your continued study as an actor, getting coaching and audition prep, etc.? Are coaches and teachers ever really worth it? Well, that depends upon whether you are currently getting work or not and whether you feel you may need some help with the work you have gotten. I work with many actors on audition preparation to help them get roles and increase their visibility, and I also work with some more established artists if they get a large break in a new role and may be a bit nervous about the role or an accent or something else within that process. I coach for stage, TV and film and work with beginners up to faces you know well. Even very well known actors have acting and accent coaches at times, often to assist with particularly hard roles or accents, or even auditions, so if you need one just take the plunge and get one. They can have a new eye on your work and pinpoint issues you did not even know were hurting you.

I often get asked about how to dress for a callback and whether you should wear the same clothes that you wore for the audition? If you noticed (whether for film or stage) a *lot* of folks auditioning and it has been a week or so since the actual audition, then you certainly could opt to wear the same clothes at the callback. You do not want the director or casting person looking for the guy in the red shirt that they loved, and you are that guy but you are now wearing a white t-shirt. I always opt to be remembered and if that means wearing the same outfit, you can bet that I do it.

What Can Really Break An Actor

Sometimes the hardest thing to deal with for an actor is not the repeated auditioning and the many rejections, but how to suffer getting through the down times, the inactive times, the times between the jobs you actually book, when you audition but nothing is happening. This may be when you think about whether or not to give it up. Maybe you were just filming a guest role on *Law & Order* and then you get nothing else for six months. That down time can be tough. If someone says that true actors never think about giving up, they are full of it. Bull. Everyone thinks about it at one time or another. But, how might you really know if this is not the career or life for you? People may say that, if you have to ask, then it is not for you. Again, I do not believe that. Everyone gets tired at times and does some soul searching. Soul searching makes you a richer person and a better artist. I left acting and went overseas for eight years and saw the world and do not ever regret it. It refreshed my worldview and made me a better actor.

However, if you have been in New York or Los Angeles and have already done all the technical requirements laid out in this book (reels, headshots, resume, etc) and have been auditioning like mad and have not gotten one callback or one role within an entire year, seriously consider either seeing an acting or audition coach, as they can pinpoint if there is something you are doing that is habitually wrong, or sincerely consider perhaps stopping acting altogether. A year is a very long time for you to be auditioning a lot and, if you have not gotten any responses in that time, then you really need to reevaluate what you are doing. (This is also when a coach can be useful, or when as an actor you want to move to the next level, get into unions or go from one line roles to guest star roles, but do not know how. A coach can often help.) Also, know that you can love something without doing it as a profession and that is alright. Even if you act for three years and then go do something else with your life, those three years will be bright in your memory and will have made you a better human being.

Always, always in your life there will be the issue of rejection. Constantly. If you are an actor then this is the life you have chosen, mostly not getting the part time and time again, broken up by occasionally getting the part. Be excited for the role you audition for, always, but not married to it or emotionally invested in it. Yes, I know this is easy to say, but I have been there and I know – get your head out of the role once your audition is over. Move on and plan to construct your life so that you have other things to move on to immediately. Print your own sides, work on them, and tear them up after each audition to let your brain feel better about letting it go. It works and it becomes an active habit of release for you. Plan for the next thing, have projects to do that you love to keep you busy and learn to distract yourself from the roles you love and were 'born' to play. You were truthfully born to play everything imaginable, and some of those roles you will get to play, but not all.

In addition to your acting and performing life, you must also get a real person's life. Travel a lot, love people, eat good food, drink, laugh, read, talk and make tons of friends. All of that 'life' stuff makes you a better, richer, happier and more interesting (and thus, much more castable) artist. It really does. Actors who only audition and memorize, and audition, and audition, and agonize over roles and audition, and audition, and wait and agonize, and audition – well, that often becomes all they do and sometimes it becomes all they are and that is not very interesting or very charismatic or very castable. I see actors like that every now and then, who constantly only audition and really have no real life or friends, and it ultimately makes them very desperate and uninteresting actors whom I would never cast. Having a good life, hobbies and people you love around you always makes you a much better artist as well as a better human being. That is what makes you sparkle in an audition and it always helps to get you cast. Remember that.

When you do finally end up getting up somewhere on a big stage in front of an applauding audience and you are accepting that big, awesome award, those of you who have worked hard and are real artists will find out, as I and many others did, that all you want to do when you are finally accepting that award is to thank others, those who supported you, those who taught you, those who cast you, those who put up with you and those who worked with you. Being an artist is never really ultimately about you, in the end. It is not about the fame. It is about the art and the work itself and all those other artists that you create it with. Be the best artist you possibly can be. I wish you the very best of luck.

RESOURCES FOR ADDITIONAL READING AND VIEWING

Books About the Craft of Acting

How to Audition on Camera by Sharon Baily

Playing Shakespeare: An Actor's Guide by John Barton

Disability & Theatre: A Practical Manual for Inclusion in the Arts by Stephanie Barton-Farcas

Shakespeare's Words by David and Ben Crystal

Awakening the Actor Within by C. Stephen Foster

Adventures in the Screen Trade by William Goldman

Which Lie did I Tell? by William Goldman

Respect for Acting by Uta Hagen

Your Film Acting Career: How to Break Into the Movies & TV and Survive in Hollywood by M. K. Lewis and Rosemary Lewis (even the most recent version may be a bit outdated, but the practical advice and sense of humor about the industry are well worth the read)

Musical Theater Auditions and Casting: A Performer's Guide from Both Sides of the Table by Neil Rutherford

Audition by Michael Shurtleff

Secrets of Screen Acting by Patrick Tucker

Playwrights Every Actor Should Read: A Good Place to Start

Stephen Adly Guirgis

Edward Albee

Maya Angelou

Peter Barnes
Samuel Beckett
Brendan Behan
John Belluso
Gurpreet Kaur Bhatti
Lee Blessing
Bertolt Brecht
Caryl Churchill
Ariel Dorfman
Lynn Dottage
Christopher Durang
Eve Ensler
John Guare
David Hare
Eugene Ionesco
Sarah Kane
Lisa Kron
Tracey Letts
David Lindsay-Abair
Suzan Lori-Parks
Craig Lucas
Terrance McNally
David Mamet
Mark Medoff
Phyllis Nagy
Marsha Norman
Eugene O'Neill
Robert Patrick
Harold Pinter
Ayn Rand
Yasmin Reza
Anthony Shaffer
Peter Shaffer
William Shakespeare (yes, all his plays)
John Patrick Shanley
Sam Shepard
Tom Stoppard

Meera Syal
Naomi Wallace
Wendy Wasserstein
Oscar Wilde
Tennessee Williams
August Wilson
Lanford Wilson

Recommended Film Viewing for All Actors

Again, this is just a start. Some of these you will find are foreign films. Often foreign films shape future US made films or are directly remade into US films and this is why these foreign classics should be watched as well.

3 Billboards Outside Ebbing, Missouri
12 Angry Men (the original)
Amarcord
Amores Perros
Apocalypse Now
Au Revoir Les Enfants
Chicago
Cinema Paradiso
Citizen Kane
The Color Purple
Day for Night
Get Out
The Godfather (and indeed the entire Godfather 'family' of films)
Gorillas in the Mist (note the 'dry cry' scene)
The Grapes of Wrath
La Strada
Life is Beautiful
Milk
Monster
Monsters Ball
Moonlight
My Left Foot

Pan's Labyrinth
The Piano (also good for young performers)
The Professional (again notable for a young Natalie Portman)
Quest for Fire
Rashomon
Shakespeare in Love
The Shape of Water
Singing in the Rain
Sophie's Choice
Taxi Driver
The Twilight Samurai
There Will be Blood
To Kill a Mockingbird
Trainspotting
The Usual Suspects
Whiplash
Who's Afraid of Virginia Woolf

For Child Actors and Their Parents
to View

This is the acting level children must compete at for film work:
The Bad Seed
Beasts of No Nation
Beasts of The Southern Wild
The Boy in the Striped Pajamas
Empire of The Sun
E.T.
The Florida Project
I Am Sam
Let the Right One In (the original, not the US remake)
Matilda
The Piano
The Professional
The Sixth Sense
Whale Rider

For Actors Looking at Motion Capture
Study or Stuntwork

Atomic Blonde

Avatar

Beowulf

The Bourne series of films

The Hobbit

Kill Bill (both volumes)

King Kong (the one starring Andy Serkis as Kong)

The Lord of the Rings trilogy

The Matrix films

Mission Impossible films

The Polar Express

Films to Watch for CGI, Blue or Green
Screen Work

The Abyss

Avatar

Cloverfield

District 9

Forrest Gump

Harry Potter series

I, Robot

Inception

The Jungle Book (live action version)

Jurassic Park series

Labrynth

Life of Pi

Men in Black series

Tron

WEBSITES AS RESOURCES

Actors Access, www.actorsaccess.com – the most comprehensive casting conglomerate online. See glossary for complete details on their company offshoots, all of which a yearly membership gives you access to.

AEA, www.actorsequity.org – the main US stage performing union.

AGMA, www.musicalartists.org – the American Guild of Musical Artists. This is made up of musicians in opera and dance primarily. Not to be confused with AFM, the American Federation of Musicians.

AGVA, www.agvausa.com – the American Guild of Variety Artists. This is made up of singers, jugglers, magicians, theme park performers and other variety artists.

The Animation Boss, theanimationboss.net – an online animation, gaming and Vfx reporter and VFX studio committed to providing the latest information, news, updates, jobs, articles, interviews, tutorials and best quality VFX services. Their commitment is to deliver the information about the latest happenings in the Indian animation industry with the passion readers have. Their Facebook page is a great illustrative look at how green screen filming works.

Backstage, www.backstage.com – the oldest casting website and the most well known in the US.

Camera Left/Stage Right, www.cameraleft.com/teachers – Cyd Strittmatter does actor training work for commercials in a collective of industry professionals who offer classes across different media platforms. If you are around the Los Angeles area this is the place to go and she is the one to see.

Charles Chessler Photography, www.charleschesslerphotography.com – a fabulously talented photographer in NYC. He can also be reached by email at charleschesslerphotography@gmail.com

Film Terms Glossary, www.filmsite.org/filmterms.html – a great comprehensive list of film slang, terminology, genres, on set terms, everything. Any young aspiring film actor should visit this site.

Hollywood Stunts, NYC, http://hollywoodstunts.com – located in Brooklyn. This is the best stunt training facility on the East Coast.

Intimacy Directors International, www.intimacydirectorsinternational.com – for directors and advocates of choreographed and controlled intimacy in performance

IBDB, www.ibdb.com – The Internet Broadway Database.

IMDb, www.imdb.com – the Internet Movie Database.

LA Stunt Training Center, www.lastunttrainingcenter.com – stunt training on the West Coast with an office in Georgia.

Nicu's Spoon, www.spoontheater.org – my company website and a good resource for disabled artists.

No Fear Shakespeare, http://nfs.sparknotes.com – the place to read and understand the Bard.

Parts Models, www.partsmodels.com – the most well known agency in the United States for 'parts' models.

The Pilot Project resource, http://hrforthearts.org – Human Resources for the Arts is the amalgamation of the vision of several New York based artists and lawyers. After some concerns regarding adequate access and implementation of necessary human resources procedures in the wake of sexual harassment issues, the New York City theater community held some informal meetings over a few months in 2017. The meetings resulted in an accumulation of information and resources, and the idea arose that it might be useful to gather this information in one spot. Thus the HR4A website was born. This site also houses the HR4A Mediation Pilot Program.

SAG-AFTRA, www.sagaftra.org – the US TV, film and radio union.

The Sawmill, www.thesawmill.ca – one of the very few motion capture studios accessible to the public in Western Canada and possibly the only facility in North America with a mandate to encompass production in motion capture, develop industry tools and engage research and development with immersive communities.

Stephanie Barton-Fracas at YouTube, www.youtube.com/channel/
    UCM6O6c6VxFXpGs-AnWvmnsw – my YouTube channel as
    an example for actors of a basic acting reel and other clips.
Volunteer Lawyers for the Arts (VLA), https://vlany.org – they offer free
    or low cost legal advice to artists and not for profit arts groups.

GLOSSARY

360 video – Also known as 'immersive videos' or even as 'spherical videos', these are video recordings where a view in every direction is recorded at the same time, being shot using an omnidirectional camera or a collection of different cameras. During playback the viewer then has complete control of the viewing direction like a panorama.

Actors Access – Casting directors have the option to release breakdowns to actors and receive submissions directly from them. Actors Access is an online casting platform where actors can view those breakdowns and submit themselves to audition for them. Actors Access is also an important tool for maintaining actors' profiles by uploading and maintaining headshots, updating their resume, adding new skills and attributes, managing performance videos and more, all online. It also includes voice over work, stunt work and other work in addition to film and theater auditions.

Actors Access Companies – A family of companies that are all included in your yearly subscription to Actors Access. Besides Actors Access itself, they are:

Breakdown Express – This is how talent representatives submit their talent via the internet and how casting staff view their submissions of those pictures, resumes and videos. After selecting talent they like, casting directors can then schedule actors as well as upload the auditions for producers and directors to review.

Showfax – This provides actors with sides. Sides are the script pages (scenes) used by actors at their audition. An annual Showfax membership not only provides free sides downloads, but also includes the ability to transmit your headshot, resume and reel for free on Actors Access. Showfax also provides actors with a discussion board, actor related resources and forums, and the ability to communicate with their guest moderators about topics that are important to actors.

Sides Express – This provides talent representatives and agents with sides. Sides are the script pages used by actors at their audition. All talent representative clients of Breakdown Services are provided with a free account on Sides Express.

Screenplay Online – This is a service used to distribute complete scripts and screenplays to actors. Users must then have the unique script codes to access the specific scripts, so the process is very secure.

Talentproplus – This is the ultimate desktop software application for talent agents and personal managers. Talentproplus is a desktop application for casting directors that automates filling in and printing all SAG-AFTRA forms, from Exhibit Es to Station 12s and Taft-Hartleys to every level of SAG-AFTRA contracts. Or the agent can choose from their own personal booking reports.

CastingAbout – This is the online casting and production guide, which tracks every major film and TV project casting in LA, and every film, TV and theater project casting in NY. Listings include each project's full casting staff and current production and casting status. Updates to the site are made daily, providing for the entertainment community the most accurate and complete snapshot of casting assignments on both coasts.

Actors' Equity Association (AEA) ('Equity') – Founded in 1913, this is the US labor union that represents more than 50,000 actors and stage managers. Equity seeks to foster the art of live theater as an essential component of society and advances the careers of its members by negotiating wages and contracts, working conditions and providing a wide range of benefits, including health and pension plans. Actors' Equity is a member of the AFL-CIO and is affiliated with FIA, an international organization of performing arts unions.

Actorgenie – Yet another app with an auditioning submission platform function. This app can also act as a log of your auditions.

ACX – ACX is an online audiobook casting and production marketplace where authors, literary agents, publishers and other rights holders can connect with narrators, engineers, recording studios and other producers capable of recording and/or producing a finished audiobook. The result: more audiobooks will be made.

ad lib – On the spot improvisations – words or gestures – that were not originally in the script or that were even added during rehearsals. These ad libs also may be requested during some auditions or callbacks. This is also known as improvisation.

ancillary rights – Contractual agreements in which a percentage of the profits from a film are received by individuals, or derived from the sale of action figures, posters, CDs, books, t-shirts, video games, etc. Actors frequently miss finding this in their contracts.

animation – The technique of photographing, drawing or electronically creating successive drawings or positions of puppets or clay figures, drawings or models within a frame to create an illusion of movement when the movie is sped up and shown as a sequence of frames.

anime – A style of animation originating in Japan that is characterized by colorful graphics depicting vibrant characters in action-filled plots, often with fantastic or futuristic themes. It is intended both for child and adult audiences.

antagonist – This character in a play or film forces change or creates conflict for the protagonist in a play or film. Often the "bad guy", but not always.

audiobook – An audio cassette, digital or CD recording of a reading of a book by a voice actor, typically a novel.

AuditionCal – A calendar app for actors and dancers in which you can track auditions, callbacks, fittings and so forth on your phone. It is very similar to an audition log.

augmented reality – An enhanced version of reality created by the use of technology to overlay digital information across an image of something being viewed through a device (such as a smartphone camera, a television or a video game screen); it is also the name of the technology used to create actual augmented reality.

Backstage – For over fifty years, beginning as a primarily theater casting platform in newspaper form, *Backstage* has been the most trusted place for actors and performers to find jobs and career advice, and for casting professionals and talent seekers to find the right performers for their projects. Today, *Backstage* is the largest online casting platform in the United States, with over 4,000 roles posted every week nationwide online, and over 100,000 members building their careers online.

blocking – The movement and positioning of actors on the stage for a theatrical production (and in film production, within the frame, called a line up).

blue screen or green screen – A blue (or green) background, in front of which moving subjects are filmed. This then allows a separately filmed background to be added digitally to the final image. Blue screen also can be used to remove part of the filmed product and digitally replace the image removed with a background or other images needed in the film.

body microphone – A small wireless microphone worn inconspicuously in an actors collar or elsewhere hidden on the actor's body and attached to a battery pack, so as to allow freedom of movement on the set or on the stage.

branding – The marketing practice of creating a name, symbol or design that identifies and differentiates a product from other products. An effective brand strategy as an actor gives you a major edge in increasingly competitive international markets.

callback – After an audition in most cases a callback means that the director liked what he or she saw in your initial audition and would like to see more in order to see what role you may fit in the show. It also usually means that, if you did not get a callback, it's thank you for coming but you will not be cast at this time.

Castivate – Castivate is another app that puts thousands of acting, singing, dancing and modeling jobs right at your fingertips. Castings that match your profile are then delivered straight to your mobile device, similar to Actors Access. You can then view the complete casting details for the project, including the submission info.

Clapit – This new app will crowdsource music, video, images, written work and other media into one place, where users will be able to 'clap' for the best examples. Friends of actors or artists will see this content first, but examples that are clapped the most will eventually be placed into a best-of feed for the community of users. It is now being touted as the hottest casting tool, merging social media popularity with casting.

cold reading – Theatrical cold reading is reading aloud from a script or other text with little or no rehearsal, practice or study in advance. It requires you to think on your feet and make immediate choices in your performance. Sometimes it is also referred to as sight reading. It is a technique used often by actors and other performers in theater, television, and the film performance fields in auditions.

commercial copy – Text of a print, radio, or television advertising message that aims to catch and hold the interest of the prospective buyer, and to persuade him or her to make a purchase, all within a few short seconds or a minute. It usually includes the product name, the brand and the tagline.

computer generated imagery (CGI) – Application of computer graphics to create or contribute to images in art, printed media, video games, films, television programs, shorts, commercials, videos and simulators of all kinds. The visual scenes may be either dynamic or static and may be two-dimensional (2D), although the term 'CGI' is most commonly used to refer to 3D computer graphics used for creating special scenes or special effects in films and television.

cripping up – Used to denote the casting and playing of disabled roles by non-disabled actors (similar to the term 'whitewashing' used to denote casting white actors in non white roles). These roles are often rewarded with accolades or awards, and touted as 'inspiring', but do true harm to the realistic representation of disabled people on film.

disk jockey (DJ) – Someone who mixes different sources of pre-existing recorded music as it is playing, usually for a live audience in a nightclub or dance club or via broadcasting, as on the radio or in podcasts.

domestic rights – Usually defined in a contract as rights to yourself on film and your likeness within the United States and English-speaking Canada.

Eco Cast® – Eco Cast is a "virtual pre-read system" provided by Breakdown Services. With it, casting directors can send invitations to talent representatives or to actors directly to invite them to record an audition themselves, hosted on the Eco Cast platform and then sent in to the casting agent, expanding the range of people that casting directors can see for each role. A membership with Actors Access allows you a free Eco Cast membership.

film frame – In filmmaking, video production, animation, and related fields, a film frame or video frame is one of the many still images that compose the complete moving picture. The term is derived from the fact that, from the beginning of modern filmmaking toward the end of the 20th century, and in many places still up to the present, the single images have been recorded on a strip of photographic film that quickly increased in length. Historically, each image on such a strip looks rather like a framed picture when examined individually.

Findaway – One of the world's largest collections of audiobooks online. They are providers of all things 'content' and they contract audiobook performers as freelance workers.

hologram – A three-dimensional image formed by the interference of numerous light beams from a laser or other coherent light source.

industrial film – A video that targets an 'industry' or a corporation as its primary audience. An industrial video is a type of sponsored film (such as an educational or training film) that prioritizes pragmatism over artistic value. While the primary purpose of an educational film is to inform or teach a corporate audience, the purpose of an industrial video can vary depending on the corporate client.

international rights – Rights to your image and likeness on film and products distributed outside of the United States and English-speaking Canada.

Internet Movie Database (IMDb) – An online database of information related to films, television programs, music videos and video games, including cast, production crew, fictional and animated characters, musicians, biographies, plot summaries, trivia and reviews, operated by IMDb.com, a subsidiary of Amazon.

iPerform – An auditioning app similar to AuditionCal.

merchandising rights – These are either domestic or international or both, and are rights to license, manufacture and distribute merchandise based on characters, names or events in a motion picture or a theatrical play or musical.

motion capture (mocap) – Process or technique of recording patterns of movement digitally, especially the recording of an actor's movements for the purpose of animating a digital character through them in a movie or for a computer game.

NDA (non-disclosure agreement) – A legally binding contract between at least two parties that outlines confidential material, knowledge, or information (spoilers) that the parties wish to share with one another for certain purposes, while restricting access to any and all third parties. It is a contract through which the parties agree not to disclose any information covered by the agreement. An NDA creates a confidential relationship between the parties to protect any type of confidential and proprietary information or trade secrets.

Offbook – Another app designed by an actor to help actors to learn lines and to be 'off book' for play or film rehearsals.

pay or play – Essentially, the commitment by a producer, a studio, network, production company or even individual to pay the artist even if the producer or director later decides that the artist's services won't be required. In other words, whether or not the production goes forward, and whether or not the artist is ultimately required to render the contracted services, he or she will still be paid the negotiated and agreed upon fee.

protagonist – The play or film revolves around this character. The leading actor, usually. Often the "good guy" but not always.

right of publicity – The right of an artist to control the commercial value and the use of one's own name, likeness, voice and image. This is one thing more actors must be cognizant of as, in an increasingly international market, it is often hard to know if your likeness is indeed being put on a bobblehead in Indonesia or a t-shirt in Kentucky without your permission or knowledge.

Scenebot – Similar to Clapit, an app that helps young actors to submit scenes to be seen by casting agents. You rehearse a scene and then you film the scene and then upload it through the app.

Scenestudy – Another app created by actors for actors. This one helps you to study lines and to work on acting scenes more easily and on the go.

Screen Actors Guild–American Federation of Television and Radio Artists (SAG-AFTRA) – SAG-AFTRA brings together two great American labor unions: the Screen Actors Guild and the American Federation of Television and Radio Artists. Both were formed in the turmoil of the 1930s, with rich histories of fighting for and securing the strongest protections for all media artists. Our members united to form the successor union in order to preserve those hard-won rights and to continue the struggle to extend and expand those protections into the 21st century and beyond. All actors who perform in filmed media that is contracted do so through this union.

SDC (Stage Directors and Choreographers Society) – The theatrical union that unites, empowers and protects professional stage directors and choreographers (both fight choreographers and dance choreographers) throughout the US.

self taped audition – Filming your audition for casting directors at your home or paying to have it taped at a facility outside of the casting office and audition schedule. It is then sent to the casting director via email or via an online service such as WeTransfer or an online casting platform such as Eco Cast.

storyboard – Graphic organizer for film or video game production in the form of illustrations or images displayed on paper or on computer in boxes in sequence for the purpose of pre-visualizing a commercial, motion picture, animation, video game or interactive media sequence. The storyboarding process, in the form it is known today, was developed at Walt Disney Productions during the early 1930s, after several years of similar processes being in use at Walt Disney and in other animation studios.

virtual reality – The computer-generated simulation of a three-dimensional image or environment that can be interacted with in a seemingly real or physical way by a person using special electronically sensitive equipment, such as a special helmet with a screen inside or with special gloves fitted with sensors.

vocaloid – A singing voice synthesizer. Its speech bank is based on a real person speaking words that are then combined and tuned to 'sing' electronically. Its signal processing part was developed through a joint research project led by Kenmochi Hideki at the Pompeu Fabra University in Barcelona, Catalonia, Spain, in 2000.

voice over – Voice over is a production technique where a voice – that is not part of the actual narrative – is used in radio, television production, filmmaking, theater or other presentations. The voice over is read from a script and recorded and may be spoken by someone who appears elsewhere in the production or by a specialist voice talent.

Volunteer Lawyers for the Arts (VLA) – Serves the artistic community's need for low cost legal services by providing access to free or low fee legal services to actors and to non profit arts organizations. Qualifying artists can request legal assistance on all arts-related legal matters.

WeTransfer – The best way to send big files to others (agents and casting staff or those who do your reels for you). This program lets you send files up to 2 GB in size to others absolutely for free. For actors needing to send larger files you may pay a subscription price.

INDEX